OCR Computing for A Level
F453 - Advanced Computing Theory
A Revision Guide

Alan Milosevic, Dorothy Williams

Published by Bagatelle Publications Ltd 2012

Published by Bagatelle Publications Ltd

http://www.bagatelle.com/

First published 2012

Printed in the United Kingdom

Set using LaTeX. Font 9pt Minion Pro.

Contents

Introduction

This revision guide has been written specifically to support work done throughout the year in F453 - Advanced Computing Theory. It is not intended to replace a good text book but when used properly will provide an excellent supplement. The revision guide is divided into chapters and sections. Each chapter and section reflect divisions in the original OCR specification for F453. Notes are distributed throughout the guide usually immediately after each section heading. These notes are then followed by a range of questions taken directly from OCR past papers, together with the examiner's mark scheme solutions. In many cases the notes are minimal since the examiner's solutions provide excellent notes.

All of the questions are taken from OCR past papers. In each instance the question number and paper are displayed together with the number of marks awarded for a fully correct answer. The answers are provided by the OCR mark scheme for the particular paper. Many of these answers are given in bullet point form. You should assume that each bullet point is worth one mark, with the proviso that if the bullet point contains an ellipsis (...), the text following the ellipsis expanding upon or providing an explanation for the first part of the text is also worth one mark.

The student who works his or her way through this book carefully reading the notes and the past paper questions and answers will give themselves an excellent opportunity to consolidate and review the material learned during the course.

The function of operating systems

1.1 Main features

Operating systems control hardware, manage peripherals, provide a Human Computer Interface (HCI), most commonly in the form of a Graphical User Interface (GUI) or command line. It also manages memory, schedules users and tasks, controls the hardware and provides a platform for applications. Memory management and scheduling algorithms are described in detail in the sections that follow.

The main features of an operating system include

- Making sure all the parts of the computer can work together
- Making sure that the user can interact with the computer by providing an interface
- Ensuring that any errors in the computer are reported to the user
- Managing memory
- Allowing the user to manage files by providing file management programs
- Providing utility programs such as *format*, or *defragment*
- Scheduling to ensure that the resources of the computer such as CPU time are used as efficiently as possible by all users and all jobs

1.2 Interrupt handling

An interrupt is an asynchronous signal indicating the need for attention or a synchronous event in software indicating the need for a change in execution.

Prior to the Fetch part of the Fetch Decode Execute (FDE) cycle, the CPU checks the contents of its interrupt register. This register tells the CPU whether an interrupt is pending and if so, the identity of the interrupt. Interrupts can be given different priorities and if the pending interrupt has higher priority than whatever it is that the CPU is currently doing (it could for example be currently servicing another interrupt), the CPU saves its current state by pushing its registers onto the stack, loads the program counter with the address of the start of relevant Interrupt Service Routine (ISR) and the FDE cycle continues from the new address. The last instruction of the ISR is invariably an Interrupt Return (IRET) instruction that restores the original CPU state by popping the saved registers from the stack and returning control to whatever the CPU was doing before it was interrupted.

It is perfectly possible for two or more interrupts to occur closely together. For example, it is perfectly possible that while the CPU is servicing a timer interrupt service request an interrupt from the printer occurs. What to do? Service the printer immediately or finish the timer interrupt and then deal with the printer? To deal with such situations, interrupts are given priority levels. More important interrupts are given higher priority.

Let us suppose that we have a situation where two tasks, both of which can generate interrupts are running. Task A is running a very long, complicated mathematical calculation.This will tie up the CPU for an extended period of time – we say that this task is processor bound. Task B meanwhile is attempting to send a file to a printer. The printer is an I/O device – this task is I/O bound. How should priorities be allocated? If task A is given higher priority, task B will not be able to interrupt the calculation and so will not be able to print until the calculation is complete - which might take many minutes, hours, or possibly much longer. However, if task B is given higher priority, it will be able to interrupt task A whenever it needs to print. Printing is limited by the speed of the printer which means that only rarely will task B actually send data to the printer. This means that only rarely is it actually in its interrupt service routine which means that task A is able to continue running most of the time. In such a situation, task B should be given higher priority.

Interrupts can come from a number of different sources; from an I/O device such as a printer or keyboard, a reset interrupt (from the reset button), a timer interrupt, or a software interrupt, generated usually by the operating system in order to obtain some CPU time for some specific reason. Invalid operations such as trying to divide by zero can also generate software interrupts.

Explain why interrupts are used in a computer system. [F453 Q1 Jan 2010 (2)]

- To obtain processor time
- ...for a higher priority task
- To avoid delays
- To avoid loss of data
- As an indicator to the processor
- ...that a device needs to be serviced

State two sources of interrupts and explain why these sources have different priorities. (1,1,2)

- (Imminent) power failure/system failure
- Peripheral e.g. printer (buffer empty)/hardware
- Clock interrupt
- User interrupt e.g. new user log on request
- Software
- Reason (related to examples chosen)
- E.g. new user can wait
- ...but data must be saved before power fails

Give one example of an interrupt that allows the job to be resumed after the system has serviced the interrupt. [F453 Q1 Specimen Questions (1)]

- Peripheral e.g. printer (buffer empty)
- User interrupt e.g. new user log on request

Describe how the system ensures that it is possible to resume the interrupted job. (2)

- Values are copied from registers
- ...and stored on the stack
- ...so they can be replaced in registers (when ISR has finished)

1.3 SCHEDULING, JOB QUEUES AND PRIORITIES

The purpose of scheduling is to

- Make efficient use of processor time
- Make efficient use of resources
- Maximise the number of users
- Ensure that there is no apparent delay for users
- Maximise throughput of the CPU

There are a number of ways of implementing scheduling. These include the 'round robin' approach in which each user and task are allocated a time slice in turn. When each user/task has been serviced the process starts over. Time slices are usually very small, of the order of a few milliseconds each, i.e. much faster than we can notice. Another approach is to simply service the most important user or task first and then service the others in descending order of priority. A third could service tasks in which the length of time each task takes is taken into account and the task with the shortest time is serviced first with the others following on in ascending lengths of time. Finally, we could adopt the 'first come - first served' approach. This last approach is most often used to manage access to a printer in which incoming print jobs are placed in a queue and are sent to the printer one after the other in the order in which they are received.

Describe two reasons why scheduling is used. [F453 Q1 Jan 2010 (4)]

- Maximise number of users
- ...with no apparent delay
- Maximise number of jobs processed
- ...as quickly as possible
- Obtain efficient use of processor time / resources
- ...dependent upon priorities
- ...to ensure all jobs obtain processor time/long jobs do not monopolise the processor

Explain why operating systems use scheduling. [F453 Q1 Specimen Questions (4)]

- Ensure all tasks are processed
- ...by changing priorities where necessary
- Process as many jobs as possible
- ...in the least possible time
- Maximise number of interactive users
- ...receiving fast response times

Round robin scheduling is one method that may be used by a multi- user operating system. Describe round robin scheduling. (3)

- Each user allocated a time slice
- When time slice is up, system moves to next user

- If next user needs processor, user given time slice
- Repeat until all users serviced
- Users may have different priorities
- Time slices are very small/fractions of seconds
- No apparent delay for any user

Describe ONE method of scheduling. [F453 Q1 Jun 2010 (2)]

- Round robin
- Each user allocated a short period of time/in a sequence

or

- System of priorities
- Highest priority first

or

- Length of job
- Shortest job first

or

- First come, first served
- Jobs are processed in order of arrival

Explain why jobs are given different priorities when in a job queue. [F453 Q1 Jan 2010 (2)]

- Some jobs are more urgent than others
- Priorities are used to maximise the use of the computer resources

1.4   MEMORY MANAGEMENT

All operating systems need to manage memory usage. Modern operating systems are multitasking and often multi-user. Each task needs its own memory space and tasks cannot be allowed to stray outside of their allocated areas. Similarly each user needs their memory space and users should not be allowed to access memory in other users' areas. The operating system prevents this from happening.

Memory is limited and when more RAM is unavailable the operating system uses a secondary storage device as additional memory. We call this 'virtual memory'. RAM is very much faster than secondary storage and when the operating system is forced to use secondary storage as RAM the system will invariably appear to run slower. If the operating system spends too much time transferring data from RAM to storage and back again the resulting slowdown can make the system unusable. This is called disk threshing.

There are two ways of using virtual memory that you need to know - *segmentation* and *paging*. Both methods make use of secondary storage as virtual memory in situations where the system has insufficient memory. They differ in the way that they do this. Paging swaps fixed size pieces of memory from RAM to secondary storage whereas segmentation swaps variable sized sections of memory. When programs are compiled and linked they can be divided up into logical sections. Where these sections start and end is visible to the operating system.

One or more of these logical sections are swapped when segmentation is used.

One feature of an operating system is memory management. State TWO reasons why memory management is necessary. [F453 Q1 Jun 2010 (2)]

- To allocate memory to allow separate processes to reside in memory and then run at the same time
- To deal with allocation when using paging or segmentation
- To reallocate memory when necessary, for example, if one program is closed, its memory space can be reallocated to other tasks.
- To protect processes and data from each other by blocking access to the code and data space of running tasks
- To protect the operating system/provide security
- To enable memory to be shared

State why virtual memory may be needed. (1)

- To allow programs to run that need more memory than is available

Describe how virtual memory is used. (3)

- Use of backing store as if it were main memory/temporary storage
- Uses paging/fixed size units
- Swaps pages between memory & backing store
- ...to make space for pages needed
- Holds part of program not in use
- Allows programs to run that need more memory than is available

Describe the problem of disk threshing. (3)

- Occurs when using virtual memory/moving pages between memory & disk
- Disk is relatively slow
- High rate of disk access
- More time spent transferring pages than on processing

An operating system may use segmentation or paging when managing memory. State two ways in which segmentation and paging are similar. [F453 Q1 Jan 2011 (1,1)]

- Both are ways of partitioning memory
- Both allow programs to run despite insufficient memory/both are used for virtual memory
- Segments and pages are both stored on backing store
- Segments and pages are assigned to memory when needed

State one difference between segmentation and paging. (1)

- Segments are different sizes but pages are fixed size
- Segments are complete sections of programs, but pages are made to fit sections of memory
- Segments are logical divisions, pages are physical divisions

Explain one problem that may occur when using paging and segmentation. (2)

- Disk threshing
- ...where more time is spent swapping pages than processing
- ...and the computer may 'hang'

1.5   SPOOLING

Spooling is an acronym for simultaneous peripheral operations on-line.[1] Spooling refers to the use of a temporary storage area, a buffer held in memory or on a disk which a device can access when it is ready. Different devices access data at different rates. Spooling allows a fast device such as a CPU to make use of a slower device such as a hard disk or a printer. In print spooling, documents are loaded into a buffer (usually an area on a disk), which the printer then accesses at its own rate. Once documents are stored in the buffer it is possible for the sending device to continue with other tasks.

One significant advantage of spooling is that it is possible to place a number of print jobs into a queue instead of waiting for each one to finish before specifying the next. It is common for print management software to manage the queue so that for example, more important documents are printed ahead of less important ones even if the less important ones got into the queue first.

In the context of printing, describe spooling and explain why it is used. [F453 Q1 Jan 2011 (4)]

- Output data to disk drive/storage device
- …for printing at another time
- To allow sharing/on a network
- Job references stored in a queue/buffer
- Avoids delays / avoids speed mismatch
- …as printers are relatively slow
- Jobs can be prioritised

1.6   MODERN PERSONAL COMPUTER OPERATING SYSTEMS

Modern personal computer operating systems have (at least) the following feature set.

- Error reporting …so you can be told about problems
- Memory management …so RAM is used efficiently
- Resources management …so resources are used efficiently
- I/O management …to look after the inputs and outputs to the computer
- Device management …so peripherals can be used
- Interrupt management …so that interrupts can be serviced
- User interface …so you can communicate with the computer

Modern personal computer operating systems often make use of *boot* files. These are read automatically by the operating system when the system starts and are used to personalise the system for the user.

In a typical desktop PC (personal computer) operating system, state when the boot file is used and what is its purpose. [F453 Q1 Jun 2011 (1,1)]

- When
  - while the operating system is loading

---

[1]webopedia

  – when the computer is switched on
  – after POST
- Purpose
  – provides personal settings

All modern operating systems have some form of file allocation table(FAT). This refers to an area on the secondary storage device where file names, the address where the first piece of data (cluster) of the file is stored, various access rights and other file details are stored. It also maintains a list of free clusters on the device. The file allocation table is used and updated whenever data is stored or retrieved from the device. It is essentially the source of all knowledge as to where data is on a given device.

Explain the purpose and use of the file allocation table (FAT). (6)

- A map of where files are stored
- …on backing store/hard disk
- Provides addresses/pointers to (start of) files
- Stores file names
- Stores file sizes
- Stores access rights
- Identifies free space
- Is updated by the operating system when files are saved and deleted
- Is used by the operating system when files are accessed

The function and purpose of translators

2.1 TYPES OF TRANSLATORS AND THEIR USE

Translators translate source code from assembler or a high level language into object code. Object code is *linked* with (perhaps) other object code and library modules to produce executable code. Loaders copy the executable code into RAM from a secondary storage device, modify memory addresses as required and point the program counter to the start of code in the newly loaded program.

Translators can be *assemblers, compilers* or *interpreters.* These are described in the sections that follow.

What is source code?

- A program written in a high level language (or in assembler)
- …by the user
- Easy for people to understand
- It cannot run until it has been
- …translated by the translator (compiler/interpreter/assembler) to object code

What is object code?

- Low level/machine code/binary code
- …used by computer
- Produced by the translator

What is executable code?

- A complete program
- …that the computer can run
- …without further translation
- Now in machine code

What is intermediate code?

- Code that has been translated usually by a compiler
- …into code that needs to be further translated (usually interpreted) before it can be run

What does the linker do?

- Combines modules/library routines
- …that are already compiled (are in object code)

What does the loader do?

- Copies modules into memory
- …from backing store
- …ready for execution
- Completes address links to the program

Various types of translator may be used when writing and preparing a new computer program. Explain the main purpose of a translator. [F453 Q2 Jun 2010 (2)]

- Convert from source code …to object code
- Detect errors in source code

Some compilers produce intermediate code instead of executable code. Explain why intermediate code may be more useful than executable code. (2)

- Can run on a variety of computers
- Same intermediate code can be obtained from different high level languages
- Improves portability

State what additional software is needed to run the intermediate code. (1)

- An interpreter / virtual machine

State one disadvantage of using intermediate code. (1)

- The program runs more slowly / has to be translated each time it is run / needs additional software

Software is used to convert source code into object code. Name this type of software. [F453 Q2 Jun 2011 (1)]

- Translator

Explain the term source code. (4)

- The original code/code written by the programmer
- …often in a high level language
- May be in assembly language
- Source code can be understood by people
- …but cannot be executed (until translated)

Some compilers produce intermediate code for a virtual machine. Explain two advantages of using intermediate code. [F453 Q2 Specimen Questions (2)]

- Intermediate code is platform-independent/may be used on a variety of machines
- Intermediate code program has been compiled so is error-free

Explain the meaning of the term virtual machine and how intermediate code is run on it. (2)

- A virtual machine is a generalised computer on which the program can run
- Intermediate code is run using an interpreter (for the specific computer)

2.2 ASSEMBLY LANGUAGE AND MACHINE CODE

Describe two differences between machine code and assembly language. [F453 Q8 Jun 2011 (4)]

- Machine code is written in binary/hexadecimal whereas assembly language
  - – is written in plain text
  - – includes mnemonics
  - – includes names for data
- Machine code needs no translation whereas assembly language
  - – is translated by an assembler
- Machine code is very difficult to write whereas assembly language
  - – is easier to write than machine code, but more difficult than a high level language

Languages used in computing include assembly language and machine code. Describe the term assembly language. [F453 Q2 Jan 2010 (2)]

- A language related closely to the computer being programmed/low level language/machine specific
- Uses descriptive names (for data stores)
- Uses mnemonics (for instructions)
- Uses labels to allow selection
- Each instruction is generally translated into one machine code instruction
- May use macros

Describe the term machine code. (2)

- Binary notation
- Set of all instructions available
- …for the architecture/which depend on the hardware design of the processor
- Instructions operate on bytes of data

The table shows statements about types of computer language. In each row, tick the box(es) to show for which type(s) of language the statement is correct. [F453 Q8 Jan 2011 (6)]

	Machine code	Assembly language	High level language
Uses mnemonics			
Uses only binary (or hexadecimal) code			
May use relative addresses			
May use local variables			
Needs translation before the program can be executed			
May be translated into intermediate code			

Answer:

	Machine code	Assembly language	High level language
Uses mnemonics		✓	
Uses only binary (or hexadecimal) code	✓		
May use relative addresses		✓	
May use local variables			✓
Needs translation before the program can be executed		✓	✓
May be translated into intermediate code			✓

2.3 THE ASSEMBLER

Assemblers are translators that convert source code written in assembly language into object code. Object modules generated by assemblers still need to be linked to produce executable code. Assembly languages are specific to a microprocessor. The instruction set of two distinct microprocessors although similar in overall concept are invariably quite different in implementation. Each microprocessor will require its own specific assembler.

Assembly language is extremely close to the instruction set of a given microprocessor. Each instruction of the instruction set of a microprocessor will have a mnemonic counterpart. Consider the following assembly language program, written in this case in Intel x86 assembly language.

```
PGROUP   Group    PROG
DGROUP   Group    DATA

DATA Segment Public 'DATA'
public brkflag
   brkflag DW    0
DATA ends

PROG Segment Para Public 'PROG'
public TrapBret
assume cs:PGROUP,DS:DGROUP

TrapBret proc near
         push ds
         push cs
         pop ds
         mov dx,offset PGROUP:Bret
         mov ah,25h
         mov al,23h
         int 21h
         pop ds
         ret
TrapBret endp

Bret proc far
         push ds
         push ax
         mov ax,DGROUP
         mov ds,ax
         mov brkflag,1
         pop ax
         pop ds
         iret
Bret endp
PROG ends
```

This short program creates two logical segments (see segmentation earlier), a data segment called 'DATA' and a code segment called 'PROG'. A single variable brkflag is defined in the data segment. The code segment has two procedures, TrapBret and Bret delimited by the words `proc` to mark the start of a procedure and `endp` to denote the end of a procedure.

The segment registers `ds` and `cs` hold the addresses of the data and code segments respectively. The first three instructions of TrapBret save `ds` and copy the contents of `cs` into the `ds` register. Segment registers cannot be copied directly, but pushing and then popping them from the stack does the job nicely. The next few instructions ending with `int 21h` set up Bret as an interrupt service routine (in this case servicing interrupt 23h). Since the original value of `ds` has been destroyed earlier the original value is popped off the stack and the procedure returns to wherever it was called.

Once `TrapBret` has run, whenever interrupt 23h (35 decimal) is triggered, subroutine/procedure `Bret` is called. Not that this is particularly interesting since all that `Bret` does is to put a 1 into the memory address specified by the variable `brkflag` which had been initialised to 0 when assembled.

When this code is assembled, the assembler will replace mnemonic opcodes and operands by binary numbers. It will replace and reserve storage for variables such as `brkflag` with its address within the data segment. It will replace symbolic addressees such as `TrapBret` and `Bret` with numeric addresses and in larger programs where routines are often written in separate files it will create a table of symbols which it will be replaced later by numeric addresses. Finally it will point out any errors in syntax.

For those interested in such things, the binary code for `push ds` is 1E or 00011110, the code for `push cs` is 0E or 00001110 whilst the code for `pop ds` is 1F or 00011111.[2] The first three instructions of `TrapBret` in machine code are therefore 00011110 00001110 00011111. Essentially, each mnemonic is translated into a single machine code instruction and if anyone was wondering why it's easier to write in assembler rather than directly in machine code here is your answer.

State three of the tasks performed by an assembler when producing machine code. [F453 Q2 Jan 2010 (3)]

- Translates a program from assembly language into machine code
- One assembly language instruction is changed into one machine code instruction
- Reserves storage for instructions and data
- Replaces mnemonic opcodes by machine codes
- Replaces symbolic addresses by numeric addresses
- Creates symbol table to match labels to addresses
- Checks syntax/offers diagnostics for errors

2.4 INTERPRETATION AND COMPILATION

When would a software developer use an interpreter and a compiler? What are the advantages and disadvantages of each?

Interpreters are often used during program development. Since interpreters translate one line at a time then run each line before translating the next line, errors can be found quickly, the

---

[2]http://ref.x86asm.net/geek32.html

program can be restarted at any point and variables and data structures inspected and modified if necessary before re-running. This means that software development is relatively fast. However, when finished, users would have to be given source code and interpreted code runs much slower than compiled code.

Compilers produce fast, optimised code and are used to generate a final executable version when programs are finished. By selling only the executable program, a purchaser has no access to the source code. However, development is usually slower using a compiler since at least one source file will need to be compiled before being linked into an executable file. Traditional development, somewhat obscured by modern Integrated Development Environments (IDEs) takes the form of Edit/Compile/Link/Run. Programmers edit one or more source files using a text editor, compile them, then link the resulting object files with (often) other object files and usually a selection of library files before finally running and testing the program. Any error will mean that the entire process has to be gone through again.

Modern IDEs obscure this process by providing an environment that allows programmers to edit their source file(s), compile and link them with a single button press and then run them using a source debugger which allows them to set breakpoints and step through the code whilst checking all the time that variables and data structures are correctly initialised and used. They blur the line between interpreters and compilers, in fact so much so that many of the advantages laid down below also apply to compiling inside a modern IDE.

The traditional advantages of using an interpreter rather than a compiler are that

- Errors are reported as they occur
- . . . rather than together
- . . . and are easier to correct
- Less memory is needed
- . . . as only the object code from a single source code instruction in use is held
- . . . and interpreters are usually smaller programs than compilers
- Programs can be restarted from any point
- . . . after correcting an error
- Breakpoints (for debugging) can be inserted in the code
- . . . to halt the program at any point
- . . . at which point the values of any variables used
- . . . can be displayed
- Similarly, it is possible to set variable values
- . . . while running the program

The disadvantages are that

- The end user needs an interpreter
- The program runs more slowly because the program has to be translated each time it is run
- The end user has to be given the source code

Either an interpreter or a compiler may be used with a high-level language program. Describe one feature of an interpreter. [F453 Q2 Jan 2010 (2)]

- Translates one line/statement
- . . . then allows it to be run before translation of next line

- Reports one error at a time
- ...and stops

State two features of a compiler. (2)

- Translates the whole program as a unit
- Creates an executable program/intermediate program
- May report a number of errors at the same time
- Optimisation

Some compilers produce intermediate code. Explain the term intermediate code and its use. [F453 Q2 Jan 2011 (3)]

- Simplified code / partly translated code
- ...which can be run on any computer/virtual machine/improves portability
- ...using an interpreter
- Sections of program can be written in different languages max
- Runs more slowly than executable code

2.5 LEXICAL ANALYSIS

Compilers are complex pieces of software and it makes good design sense to consider compiling as three distinct processes, called respectively, *Lexical Analysis*, *Syntax Analysis* and *Code Generation*. The output from the lexical stage is fed into the syntax stage and the output from the syntax stage is fed directly into the code generation phase. If errors have not occurred in any of the three stages, the code generation phase will output an object file which can be later linked with other object files and library modules to produce an executable file.

Each of the three stages have very specific jobs. Lexical analysis takes the source program, strips out comments and whitespace (spaces, carriage returns and line feeds) and replaces reserved words and symbols used in the program with tokens (fixed length strings of binary digits). Variable names are stored for later use and error messages are output if necessary. The resulting stream of tokens is fed into the syntax analysis stage.

To illustrate what this means in practice, consider the following trivial code example, with the caveat that this is a very much simplified description.

```
// Simple test to set flag appropriately
 IF A > B THEN
    flag = TRUE;
 ELSE
    flag = FALSE;
```

During the lexical stage comments and whitespace are removed leaving the following.

```
IFA>BTHENflag=TRUE;ELSEflag=FALSE;
```

Each of the reserved words (IF, THEN, ELSE, TRUE, FALSE), variables (A,B,flag), mathematical operators(>=) and punctuation (;) are removed and replaced by tokens, i.e. numbers which might give us the denary sequence

40 20 35 20 41 20 97 121 17 42 20 97 120 17[3]

In this simple example, IF has been replaced by token number 40 , A by 20, > by 35, B by 20, THEN by 41 and so on.

You might object that whereas IF, THEN, > etc. have been replaced with unique token codes, A, B and flag have each been replaced by the same number, in this case 20. This is correct, but as far as the syntax analysis stage is concerned this is unimportant. However, of course we do somehow need to keep track of what variable we are using at each point in the program so in addition to replacing each variable by token number 20, each of the variables is entered into a lookup table together with its position(s) in the token stream. The lookup table will then be used during the code generation phase to replace variable A with its newly allocated (at code generation time) memory address.

Very few errors are detected at the lexical analysis stage. Characters not in the language character set might be detected during the lexical stage as might over long strings but that's about it. Most errors are found during the syntax analysis stage.

One stage of compilation is lexical analysis. Describe what happens during lexical analysis. (The quality of written communication will be assessed in your answer to this question.) [F453 Q2 Jan 2010 (8)]

Points to be made include:

- Source program is used as the input
- Tokens are created from individual symbols and from
- ...the reserved words in the program
- A token is a fixed length string of binary digits
- Variable names are loaded into a look-up table / symbol table
- Redundant characters (eg spaces) are removed
- Comments are removed
- Error diagnostics are given
- Prepares code for syntax analysis

2.6 SYNTAX ANALYSIS

The incoming stream of tokens from lexical analysis is read and checked to ensure that it conforms to the rules of the language being used. If there are no errors the stream is passed to the code generation phase otherwise errors are reported to the user.

If we take the artificial token stream generated according to my coding scheme above, the syntax stage receives the token stream 40 20 35 20 41 20 97 121 17 42 20 97 120 17 which it will then attempt to match to the rules of the language. The token stream says that

```
IF variable operator variable THEN variable equals boolean semicolon ELSE
variable equals boolean semicolon
```

---

[3]I am using denary here only for brevity.   In reality, the stream of tokens would look like 00101000000101000010001100010100 ...

which in languages based on C is perfectly valid. If on the other hand the token stream was 40 20 35 20 41 20 97 121 42 20 97 120, this token stream is missing the semi-colons which are required in C based languages and an error would be generated.

Similarly, if a reserved word is mis-spelled, for example THNE instead of THEN, the lexical analysis stage might legitimately assume that THNE was a variable and would tokenise it appropriately (with 20 instead of 41 in my simple coding scheme). In this case the syntax analysis stage would read a token stream of 40 20 35 20 20 20 97 121 17 42 20 97 120 17 which means

```
IF variable operator variable variable variable equals boolean semicolon
ELSE variable equals boolean semicolon
```

which is clearly an error in most languages.

Describe what happens during syntax analysis. [F453 Q2 Jan 2011 (5)]

- Accepts output from lexical analysis
- Statements/arithmetic expressions/tokens are checked
- ...against the rules of the language/valid example given e.g. matching brackets
- Errors are reported as a list (at the end of compilation)
- Diagnostics may be given
- If no errors, code is passed to code generation
- Further detail is added to the symbol table
- ...e.g. data type /scope/address

One stage of compilation is syntax analysis. Give the correct name for each of the other two stages. [F453 Q2 Jan 2011 (2)]

- Lexical analysis
- Code generation

2.7 CODE GENERATION AND OPTIMISATION

Code generation produces machine code/executable code. Several instructions are usually produced for each high level language instruction. All variables are given addresses, all constants are given addresses and relative addresses are calculated. In addition, code can be optimised.

Most compilers have various optimisation options. For example it is possible to optimise for speed or for code size or for a variety of other esoteric options. Counter intuitively perhaps, optimising for speed can often result in a larger program since if asked to optimise for speed a compiler might replace multiple calls to small functions with code for the small function at each point that the call is made. This will increase the size of the code but will save the time spent pushing and popping addresses and parameters onto and off the stack.

When a compiler is used to produce executable code, code generation includes optimisation. Describe what optimisation does. [F453 Q2 Jun 2010 (2)]

- Makes code as efficient as possible

- Increases processing speed
- Reduces number of instructions

Complete the table with ticks to show at which stage, if any, events occur when a compiler is used. [F453 Q2 Jun 2011 (6)]

	Lexical analysis	Syntax analysis	Code generation	Not during compilation
Optimisation occurs				
Logical errors are detected				
Tokens are created				
Spaces are removed				
Comments are removed				
Incorrect punctuation is detected				

Answer:

	Lexical analysis	Syntax analysis	Code generation	Not during compilation
Optimisation occurs			✓	
Logical errors are detected				✓
Tokens are created	✓			
Spaces are removed	✓			
Comments are removed	✓			
Incorrect punctuation is detected		✓		

2.8   LIBRARY ROUTINES

The number of keywords used in computer languages are surprisingly small. (C has typically 32, C++ around 80). The power and sophistication of a program comes from combining such words to create subroutines, i.e. functions and procedures that the programmer creates while constructing his or her program. Companies that produce compilers invariably also release a set of libraries (also called frameworks) which provide a wide range of useful functions that the programmer can drawn upon. Modern compilers have libraries that provide thousands of such additional functions.

These functions are extensively tested before release and can usually be relied upon to produce efficient, correct code. They significantly enhance the programmer's ability to write complex programs and most of today's sophisticated applications simply would not exist without their use.

Compilation is the process by which a source file is converted into an object file. Most programs consist of a number of source files and each file typically makes calls to functions provided by external libraries. When all source files have been compiled, they are *linked* to produce an executable file. The link process reads each object file, makes a note of any external functions called by the file and searches the library files for the appropriate functions. When linking is done statically, code for the called function is copied from the library and added to the growing executable file. When all called functions have been found and added to the file the link process completes and the programmer is left with an executable file. If any external functions are not found the linker produces an appropriate error message.

When the programmer wants to run an executable program he or she clicks on an icon or types the name of the program on the command line. This causes the *loader* to run. The loader places the executable file into memory, resolves any relocatable addresses in the file and passes command to the start of the program code.

Describe what is meant by a library routine and their use when producing programs.[F453 Q2 Specimen Questions (4)]

- Piece of software
- Routines often perform common tasks
- Routines are compiled
- Routines are error-free
- Available to programmer to use with a new program

Describe how library routines are used when producing software. (3)

- May allow programmer to use code which was written in a different (source) language
- Linker is used to link the routine to the program
- Standard routines for sorting/searching available
- Allow programmer to use others expertise
- Fit into modularisation of algorithm
- May be used multiple times
- The loader will handle addresses when loaded

When producing programs, library routines may be used. Explain why library routines help programmers and describe how library routines are used. (The quality of written communication will be assessed in your answer to this question.) [F453 Q2 Jun 2011 (8)]

The examiners expected answers to include the following points.

- Library routines
    - are pieces of software
    - ...which perform common tasks
    - ...such as sorting/searching
    - routines are compiled
- Why library routines help programmers
    - routines are error-free/have already been tested
    - already available/ready to use/saves work/saves time
    - routines may be used multiple times
    - routines may have been written in a different source language
    - allows programmer to use others' expertise
- How routines are used
    - linker is used
    - ...to link routine with program
    - loader handles addresses
    - ...when program is to be run

Computer architectures

3.1 Von Neumann architecture

This standard computer architecture was first suggested in a report prepared by mathematician John von Neumann in 1945 in which he outlined a computer system comprised of a single execution unit that fetched, decoded and executed instructions one at a time and where code and data shared the same format and memory space.

State the three stages, in order, of the machine cycle in classic Von Neumann architecture. [F453 Q3 Jan 2010 (2)]

- Fetch
- Decode
- Execute

One feature of Von Neumann architecture is the use of the fetch-execute cycle. State TWO other features of Von Neumann architecture. [F453 Q3 Jun 2010 (2)

- Single control unit/processor (manages program control)
- Program stored with data in the same format
- One instruction at a time

3.2 Registers – purpose and use

All modern Von Neumann microprocessors incorporate a number of memory registers. These are small pieces of RAM that are used to store data temporarily whilst the microprocessor is in operation. 32 bit CPUs have registers 32 bits wide, 64 bit CPUs have registers 64 wides and so on. Some registers are general purpose and many instructions can operate on them. Others are specialised for particular tasks and have a small number of instructions associated with them. For example, in Intel CPUs the EAX and EBX registers are general purpose and both registers can be used by the majority of instructions. The SI and DI index registers are typically used together in moving the contents of memory locations pointed to by the SI register to memory pointed to by the DI register.

All microprocessors have a *program counter* (alternatively called the *instruction pointer*) that points to the next instruction to be executed. All have a *flags* register, a group of bits that are set or reset depending upon certain conditions in the CPU. All have at least one *accumulator* or general purpose register. All have an *interrupt* register – a register which tracks if and which interrupt has been triggered. All of these registers are available to programmers specialising in low level coding.

In addition to these there are registers that act behind the scenes and are not explicitly programmable. These are used in the fetch–decode–execute cycle and include the *Memory Data Register (MDR)*, the *Memory Address Register (MAR)* and the *Current Instruction Register (CIR)*.

In classic Von Neumann architecture, a number of registers are used. Explain the term register. [F453 Q3 Jan 2011 (2)]

- A location in the processor
- Used for a particular purpose
- (Temporarily) stores data/or control information max
- Explained example of contents held by named register

The program counter is one register used by the processor. Give the names of THREE other registers used by the processor. (Do not use abbreviations) [F453 Q3 Jun 2010 (3)]

- Memory address register
- Memory data register
- Current instruction register
- Accumulator
- Interrupt register
- Index register

3.3   Fetch-execute cycle

Von Neumann microprocessors operate a fetch-decode-execute cycle where instructions are fetched, decoded, executed and the process repeated from switch-on to switch-off. In simple terms, the contents of the program counter, which always holds the address of the next instruction to be executed, is copied into the memory address register. The program counter can now be incremented to point to the next instruction. Meanwhile the instruction held in the location pointed at by the memory address register can be brought across the data bus into the memory data register which immediately copies it into the current instruction register for decoding and subsequent execution. The sequence then starts over.

If when decoding the instruction it transpires that the instruction is actually a jump command, the address part of the jump instruction is copied into the program counter so that the next instruction is fetched from the new location.

Describe the fetch-execute cycle. [F453 Q3 Jun 2010 (4)]

- PC holds address of next instruction
- Copy contents of PC to MAR
- Increment PC
- Load instruction pointed to by the MAR to MDR
- Copy instruction from MDR to CIR
- Decode instruction in CIR

Describe how a jump instruction is executed. (2)

- By changing contents of PC (to address part of instruction)
- Copy address part of instruction
- ...in the CIR to the PC

Describe the effects of the fetch-execute cycle on the program counter (PC) and the memory address register (MAR). [F453 Q3 Jun 2011 (5)]

- PC holds address of next instruction
- PC passes this address to MAR
- MAR holds address of instruction/data
- Instruction/data from address in MAR is loaded to MDR
- PC is incremented (in each cycle)
- PC is changed when there is a jump instruction
- ...by taking address from instruction in CIR

3.4 OTHER MACHINE ARCHITECTURES

There are other computer architectures in common use. These include the use of additional processors which run in parallel with the main processor and array processors which can execute a single instruction on multiple pieces of data simultaneously. In future years quantum computer systems will be added to this section, but not quite yet.

Computer scientists have spent much time and effort trying to improve the throughput of computer systems. A simple approach is to add additional processors, often called co-processors to perform very specific tasks. Examples would include mathematics co-processors, designed to perform complex floating point instructions very rapidly whilst the main processor can get on with other things and graphics processors designed to do the highly intensive and complex mathematical instructions necessary to perform shading and shadowing in 3D applications. In each case the main processor sends a high level instruction to the co-processor and then carries on immediately with other instructions. When the co-processor receives the high level command which might (in very simple terms) be to shade a particular object in a 3D game, it performs a series of mathematical shading algorithms to implement the command. The graphics processor is designed to execute such algorithms in the most efficient fashion possible and can do so far faster than the main processor, which invariably is a very general purpose processor designed to perform a range of simple tasks.

The most powerful computer systems in use today are examples of parallel processing where many thousands of microprocessors are connected together to perform tasks ranging from nuclear fusion simulations to weather forecasting. Each processor runs a piece of the whole program simultaneously with every other processor. Such parallel systems can, when appropriate software is written for them solve problems in a sensible time frame that simply could not be done in any reasonable time if run on a single processor. However, it can be very difficult to write such software, the operating system can be very complex and synchronisation of all of the processors can be difficult to manage.

Microprocessors found in modern personal computers can contain two, four or more execution units in a single microprocessor package. In such systems, instructions can execute in parallel but for maximum benefit software needs to be written specifically to take advantage of such units. As they have become more and more common this is increasingly the case today.

Array processors are SIMD (Single Instruction Multiple Data) processors that are designed to execute one instruction on several data items simultaneously. The two diagrams[4] shown below illustrate the functional difference between a typical microprocessor and an array processor.

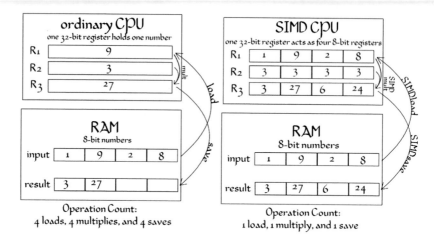

This left hand diagram shows the ordinary tripling of four 8-bit numbers. The CPU loads one 8-bit number into R1, multiplies it with R2, and then saves the answer from R3 back to RAM. This process is repeated for each number.

The right hand diagram shows the SIMD tripling of four 8-bit numbers. The CPU loads 4 numbers at once, multiplies them all in one SIMD-multiplication, and saves them all at once back to RAM. In theory, the speed up is about 75%.

In some computer systems, a co-processor may be used. Explain the term co-processor.
[F453 Q3 Jun 2010 (3)]

- An additional processor
- ...used for a specific task
- Improves processing speed by executing concurrently
- E.g. maths co-processor/floating point accelerator

Describe parallel processing. [F453 Q3 Specimen Questions (5)]

- More than one processor ...
- ...controlled by a complex operating system
- Working together
- ...to perform a single job
- ...which is split into tasks
- Each task may be performed by any processor

---

[4]http://en.wikipedia.org/wiki/SIMD

Describe one advantage and one disadvantage of a parallel processor compared with a single processor system. (2)

- Advantage
    - Increased speed/multiple instructions processed at once
    - Complex tasks performed efficiently
    - Allows faster processing
    - More than one instruction (of a program) is processed at the same time
    - Different processors can handle different tasks/parts of same job
- Disadvantage
    - Not suitable for some programs
    - Programs written specially/may need to be rewritten
    - Operating system is more complex
    - ...to ensure synchronisation
    - Program has to be written in a suitable format
    - Program is more difficult to test/write/debug

Explain, with the aid of an example, the following statement: 'A co-processor is a simple form of parallel processor.' (2)

- A component added to the central processor
- Improves speed by performing certain tasks
- E.g. maths co-processor/floating-point accelerator
- E,g. graphics co-processor

Explain the term array processor. [F453 Q3 Jan 2010 (2)]

- A processor that allows the same instruction to operate simultaneously
- ...on multiple data locations
- The same calculation on different data is very fast
- Single Instruction Multiple Data (SIMD)

Give one example of the type of task for which an array processor is most suitable. (1)

- E.g. weather forecasting / airflow simulation around new aircraft

Discuss the use of different computer architectures for different problem solutions. (The quality of your written communication will be assessed in your answer to this question) [F453 Q3 Specimen Questions (8)]

The examiners expected the following points to be included.

- Von Neumann architecture
    - Involves the use of data and instruction being held together in memory
    - Sequential processing
    - Involves the use of a sequence of instructions carried out in a specific order to solve a problem
    - Following a specific algorithm
    - Where the order will change the outcome
    - Suits any example where the outcome is dependent on steps being taken in a defined order e.g. the solution to a formula
    - Necessarily time hungry because it uses a single processor

- Parallel processing
    - Uses multiple processors
    - ...to carry out instructions at the same time
    - Requires complex processing to adapt the sequential algorithm
    - Speeds up arithmetic processes
    - Mention of co-processing
- Array processing
    - Used in time dependent operations which require large amounts of processor time
    - E.g. weather forecasting

3.5   RISC, CISC

RISC and CISC are two fundamentally different approaches to microprocessor design. CISC (Complex Instruction Set Computing) processors typically have many hundreds of instructions in their instruction set of which many may execute several low level operations to complete their instruction. They have a wide variety of addressing modes and can also include array processing instructions. Because of their complexity, the most complex CISC instructions can take many dozens of clock cycles to complete.

RISC (Reduced Instruction Set Computing) processors have a relatively small instruction set and each instruction is designed to complete its operation ideally in a single clock cycle. Because of this each RISC processor instruction typically performs a single relatively simple operation. Consequently, many instructions are sometimes required to execute tasks performed by a single CISC instruction.

Two computer architectures are Reduced Instruction Set Computer (RISC) and Complex Instruction Set Computer (CISC) architectures. Complete the table to show how the statements apply to these architectures. (tick the appropriate boxes) [F453 Q3 Jan 2010 (4)]

	RISC only	CISC only	both RISC and CISC
Has many addressing modes			
Many instructions available			
Uses one or more register sets			
Uses only simple instructions			

Answer:

	RISC only	CISC only	both RISC and CISC
Has many addressing modes		✓	
Many instructions available		✓	
Uses one or more register sets			✓
Uses only simple instructions	✓		

Compare the number of machine cycles used by RISC and CISC to complete a single task. (2)

- RISC – each task may take many cycles
- CISC – a task may be completed in a single cycle
- ...as instructions may be more complex than individual instructions in RISC

State three features of a Complex Instruction Set Computer (CISC) architecture. [F453 Q3 Jun 2011 (3)]

- Uses (complex) instructions each of which may take multiple cycles
- Single register set
- Instructions have variable format
- Many instructions are available
- Many addressing modes are available

Explain one disadvantage, other than cost, of a CISC architecture compared with a Reduced Instruction Set Computer (RISC) architecture. (2)

- Programs run more slowly
- ...due to the more complicated instructions/circuit

4

4

Data representation

4.1 FLOATING POINT BINARY

Floating point numbers can be represented in binary form in which numbers are expressed as a non zero binary or fractional value called the *mantissa*, together with an integer *exponent*. Exam questions often assume that 8 bits are used in the representation and stipulate how many bits are used for each.

The following exam questions and mark scheme answers show clearly how to convert from denary into a given floating point binary representation and backwards.

A real binary number may be represented in normalised floating point binary notation using 5 bits for the mantissa and 3 bits for the exponent, both in two's complement binary.

Convert the following binary number to denary. Show your working. [F453 Q4 Specimen Questions (3)]

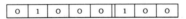

- Exponent 100 represents -4
- Mantissa 0.1, move point 4 places left so becomes 0.00001
- Value is $\frac{1}{32}(= 0.03125)$

or

- Exponent 100 represents -4
- Mantissa 0.1 represents $\frac{1}{2}$
- Value is $\frac{1}{2}$ multiplied by $2^{-4} = \frac{1}{32}(= 0.03125)$.

Write the denary number +5 in this binary format. Show your working. (3)

- 5 in pure binary = 101
- Normalised, we get 0.101, point moved 3 places
- So the exponent is 3 written as 011
- Giving us the final 8 bit byte 01010 011

Write, in this format, the largest (positive) binary number that can be represented. (1)

- 01111 011

29

Give the denary equivalent of this largest (positive) binary number. (1)

- 111.1 equivalent to 7.5

A real binary number may be represented in normalised floating point binary notation using 5 bits for the mantissa and 3 bits for the exponent, both in two's complement binary.

Convert the following binary number to denary. Show your working. [F453 Q4 Jan 2010 (3)]

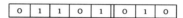

- Exponent 010 represents 2
- Mantissa 0.1101, move point 2 places right so becomes 011.01
- Value is 3.25

or

- Exponent 010 represents 2
- Mantissa 0.1101 represents $\frac{13}{16}$ $(= 0.8125)$
- Value is $\frac{13}{16}$ multiplied by $2^2 = \frac{13}{4} = 3.25$

Convert the following binary number to denary. Show your working. (3)

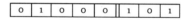

- Exponent 101 represents -3
- Mantissa 0.1, move point 3 places left so becomes 0.0001
- Value is $\frac{1}{16}$ $(= 0.0625)$

or

- Exponent 101 represents -3
- Mantissa 0.1 represents $\frac{1}{2}$ $(= 0.5)$
- Value is $\frac{1}{2}$ multiplied by $2^{-3} = \frac{1}{16}$ $(= 0.0625)$

A real binary number may be represented in normalised floating point binary notation using 6 bits for the mantissa and 2 bits for the exponent, both in twos complement binary.

Convert the following binary number to denary. Show your working. [F453 Q4 Jun 2010 (3)]

| 0 | 1 | 0 | 1 | 1 | 0 || 0 | 1 |

- Exponent 01 represents 1
- Mantissa 0.10110, move point 1 place right so becomes 01.0110
- Value is 1.375

Or

- Exponent 01 represents 1
- Mantissa 0.10110 represents $\frac{11}{16}$ or 0.6875
- Value is $\frac{11}{16}$ multiplied by $2^1 = \frac{11}{8} = 1.375$

Write, in binary, the largest positive number that can be represented in this format. (2)

- The mantissa is 011111
- The exponent is 01 so the answer is 01111101
  (equivalent to $1 + \frac{1}{2} + \frac{1}{4} + \frac{1}{8} + \frac{1}{16} = 1.9375$)

A real binary number may be represented in floating point binary notation using 5 bits for the mantissa and 3 bits for the exponent, both in twos complement binary. Three numbers P, Q and R are written in the format described but are not normalised.

- P = 00100 010
- Q = 00010 011
- R = 00001 100

By converting each of P, Q and R to denary, show which represents a different value. Show all working. [F453 Q4 Jan 2011 (4)]

- P
  - mantissa 0.010
  - exponent 010 = 2
  - binary value is 1 therefore denary value is 1
- Q
  - mantissa 0.001
  - exponent 011 = 3
  - binary value is 1 therefore denary value is 1
- R
  - mantissa 0.0001
  - exponent 100 = -4
  - binary value is 0.00000001 therefore denary value is $\frac{1}{256}$
- Consequently, R represents a different value

A real binary number may be represented in floating point binary notation using 4 bits for the mantissa and 4 bits for the exponent, both in twos complement binary. Numbers are normalised. Convert 0110 0010 to denary. Show all working. [F453 Q4 Jun 2011 (3)]

- Exponent 0010 = 2
- Mantissa 0.11, move point 2 places to right = 011
- Denary value is $(2 + 1) = +3$

Convert 1001 0001 to denary. Show all working. (3)

- Exponent 0001 = 1
- Mantissa 1.001, move point 1 place to right = 10.01
- Denary value is $-2 + \frac{1}{4} = -\frac{13}{4}$ (or -1.75)

Using 5 bits for the mantissa and 3 bits for the exponent, convert the denary number +2.25 to a normalised floating point binary number. Show all working. [F453 Q4 Jan 2011 (3)]

- 2.25 = 010.01 in pure binary
- Move point 2 places to left

- Mantissa is 01001
- Exponent is 010
- Answer is 01001 010

Convert the denary number +3.5 to binary, giving your answer as a normalised floating point number using 4 bits for the mantissa and 4 bits for the exponent. Show your working.
[F453 Q4 Jun 2010 (3)]

- +3.5 in binary 11.1 giving us 011.1
- Mantissa is 0111 (move point 2 places left)
- Exponent is 0010 (for 2, fill with 0s to get 4 bits)
- Answer : 0111 0010

4.2 NORMALISATION

In order to ensure that each floating point number has a unique floating point representation it is normalised by adjusting the exponent so that the binary representation starts with a 01 if positive or 10 if negative.

State the format of the mantissa of a normalised floating point binary number. [F453 Q4 Jan 2011 (1)]

- (Exponent is adjusted so that mantissa) starts 01 or 10

Give the normalised version of the number 00010 011 where 5 bits are used for the mantissa and 3 bits for the exponent. (2)

- Answer is 01000 001
- (Mantissa 00010, move point 2 places) 01000
- (Exponent) 001

Floating point numbers may be represent by 4 bits for the mantissa and 4 bits for the exponent. Two numbers have been written in binary. Only one of the numbers has been normalised.

Number A

| 1 | 0 | 0 | 1 || 0 | 1 | 1 | 0 |

Number B

| 0 | 0 | 1 | 1 || 1 | 0 | 1 | 0 |

State which of the numbers has been normalised giving a reason for your answer. [F453 Q4 Jun 2010 (1)]

- A, as first 2 bits are different/starts with 10

Give TWO reasons why binary numbers should be normalised. (2)

- To ensure unique representation of a number
- To provide maximum precision/accuracy
- Multiplication is more accurate

4.3   ACCURACY AND RANGE

In a given representation, increasing the number of bits in the mantissa at the expense of the exponent increases accuracy at the expense of range. Conversely, increasing the number of bits in the exponent at the expense of the mantissa increases range, but decreases accuracy. This is shown in the following two short tables which show the result of changing a representation of 5 bits for mantissa, 3 bits for exponent (5:3)

0	1	1	1	1	0	1	1	i.e. $0.1111 \times 2^3 = 111.1 = 7.5$
0	1	1	1	0	0	1	1	i.e. $0.1110 \times 2^3 = 111.0 = 7.0$
0	1	1	0	1	0	1	1	i.e. $0.1101 \times 2^3 = 110.1 = 6.5$
0	1	1	0	0	0	1	1	i.e. $0.1100 \times 2^3 = 110.0 = 6.0$

into 4 bits for mantissa, 4 bits for exponent (4:4). In each representation the four largest positive numbers are shown.

0	1	1	1	0	1	1	1	i.e. $0.111 \times 2^7 = 1110000 = 112$
0	1	1	0	0	1	1	1	i.e. $0.110 \times 2^7 = 1100000 = 96$
0	1	0	1	0	1	1	1	i.e. $0.101 \times 2^7 = 1010000 = 80$
0	1	1	0	0	1	1	1	i.e. $0.100 \times 2^7 = 1000000 = 64$

With 5 bits for the mantissa and 3 bits for the exponent, the largest number we can express is 7.5 with each subsequent number smaller by 0.5. With 4 bits for each of the mantissa and exponent we can now express 112 in this format, but the gap between subsequent numbers is now 16. By moving from 5:3 to 4:4 we have gained range but at the expense of accuracy.

Explain what happens when the denary number $+5\frac{1}{4}(+5.25)$ is converted to a normalised floating point binary number when 4 bits are used for the mantissa and 4 bits are used for the exponent. [F453 Q4 Jun 2011 (4)]

- $+5\frac{1}{4} = 101.01$ in pure binary
- Mantissa is 010101, but only 4 bits allowed
- …so mantissa would be 0101 (5 stored, not $5\frac{1}{4}$)
- Value stored is inaccurate/precision lost
- Exponent is 0011
- Number would be stored as 01010011

Floating point binary numbers may be represented by 5 bits for the mantissa and 3 bits for the exponent. If, instead, 4 bits are used for the mantissa and 4 bits for the exponent, state the effect on the range and accuracy of the numbers that can be represented. [F453 Q4 Specimen Questions (2)]

- Accuracy decreased (as fewer bits available)
- Range increased (as larger magnitude exponent available)

Floating point binary numbers may be represented by 5 bits for the mantissa and 3 bits for the exponent. If, instead, 3 bits are used for the mantissa and 5 bits for the exponent, state the effect on the range and accuracy of the numbers that can be represented. [F453 Q4 Jan 2010 (2)]

- Larger range
- Values less accurate

Consider the normalised floating point number 01111 011 in which 5 bits represent the mantissa and 3 bits for the exponent. Explain why this number is important. [F453 Q4 Jan 2011 (2)]

- Maximum (positive) number in this format
- As mantissa & exponent each have their largest values

Data structures and data manipulation

5.1 IMPLEMENTATION OF DATA STRUCTURES

An array is a static data structure. Arrays can be used to represent dynamic data structures such as stacks and queues. A static data structure has a fixed size that cannot change during processing. Static data structures are easier to program and since the amount of storage required is known in advance, this is often an advantage. Dynamic data structures are of variable size and the size will invariably change during the course of the program. In situations where the memory requirements are not known in advance, it is clearly an advantage to use dynamic data structures. A *stack* is a Last In First Out (LIFO) data structure. It needs one pointer to the top of the stack. Data is *pushed* onto the stack and *popped* off it. A *queue* is a First In First Out (FIFO) data structure. It needs two pointers, one (the start pointer) to the first item in the queue, the second (the end pointer) to the next available free space.

To add data to a queue

- Check for a full queue
- ...and report an error if it is full
- Move the end pointer to point to the new item
- ...and insert the new data item at the end of the queue

To remove data from a queue

- Check for an empty queue
- ...and report an error if it is empty
- Else, remove data pointed to by the front pointer
- ...and move the front pointer to the next item

A *binary tree* structure is composed of nodes. All nodes have at most two nodes coming off them. When constructing a binary tree from a data stream, one first creates the *root* node. This node holds the first item in the stream. Subsequent items are added to the tree in the following manner.

- Start at root
- Repeat
- ...compare new data with current data
- ...if new data < current data, follow left pointer
- ...else follow right pointer
- Until pointer is null

- Write new data
- Create (null) pointers for new data

To delete items from a tree...

- Traverse tree until item is found
- ...and remove elements below item
- ...store them
- Delete item
- Transfer stored items back onto tree

To traverse a binary tree, *in-order* traversal is

- traverse left subtree
- visit root
- traverse right subtree

A tree is a dynamic data structure. State the meaning of the term dynamic when applied to data structures. [F453 Q5 Jan 2011 (1)

- Size changes as data is added & removed/size is not fixed

State one disadvantage to the programmer of using dynamic data structures compared with static data structures. (1)

- More complex/difficult program to write

State one type of data structure which must be static.

- Array/fixed length record

Draw a diagram to show the binary sort tree obtained by adding the words orange, red, yellow, pink, green, blue to an empty tree in the order given so that they can be sorted into alphabetical order. (3)

Answer:

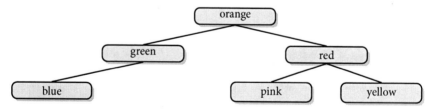

List the steps needed to add one new data item to an existing binary tree, stating any assumptions you make. (6)

The examiners were looking for something along the lines of the following.

```
start at root
repeat
  compare new data with current data
  if new data < current data, follow left pointer
  else follow right pointer
```

```
until pointer is null
write new data
create (null) pointers for new data
```

Marks were awarded for :

- Start at root
- Repeat until loop/while loop
- Comparison of values
- Follow pointers
- Condition for end of loop
- Writing data
- Creating new pointers
- Assume new data item is not already in binary tree / is same data type

The diagram shows a data structure storing data items A, B and C. Two pointers are used:

front   points to the first item in the structure
free   points to the free space immediately after the structure

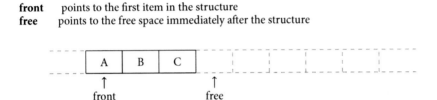

Data items can only be removed from the front of the structure, while data items must be added to the other end. State the correct name for this type of data structure. (1)

- A queue

Complete the diagram below to show the result of removing one data item and adding two new data items X and Y in that order. (3)

Answer:

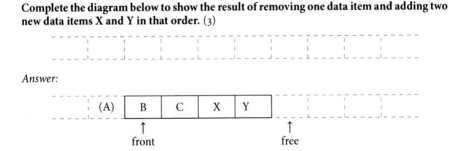

The examiner awarded marks for the following.

- Front pointer moved to B
- X in cell to right of C and Y in cell to right of X
- Free pointer moved to correct position

An array is an example of a static data structure. State the meaning of the term static in this context. [F453 Q5 Jun 2010 (1)]

- Size is fixed when structure is created/size cannot change during processing

State ONE advantage of using a static data structure compared with a dynamic data structure. (1)

- Amount of storage is known/easier to program

The diagram shows a data structure storing data items A, B and C. Two pointers are used:

front   points to the first item in the structure
free   points to the free space immediately after the structure

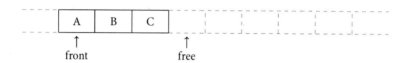

Complete the diagrams below to show the result of each change. For each example, you should start from the original queue. Two items are removed from the queue. [F453 Q5 Specimen Questions (1)]

Answer:

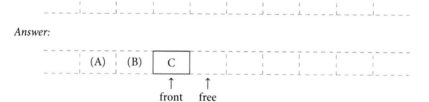

One item D is added to the original queue. (1)

Answer:

The queue shown earlier is a dynamic data structure. State the meaning of the term dynamic in this context. (1)

- Size changes as data is added and removed/size is not fixed

A queue data structure could be represented by a circular queue. For example:

Explain why this representation of a queue may be more efficient. (2)

- Easier to program (because fixed size)
- All available storage may be re-used

Describe the situation in which the free and front pointers have the same value. (1)

- Queue is empty

A stack contains a number of data items. List the steps needed to attempt to add one data item to the stack. [F453 Q5 Jan 2010 (3)

- If stack is full
- …report error and stop
- Else increment pointer
- Add data item at pointer

List the steps needed to pop a data item from a stack data structure. [F453 Q5 Jun 2011 (3)]

- If stack is empty
- …report error and stop
- Output data(stack-pointer)
- Decrement stack-pointer

5.2 SEARCHING, MERGING AND SORTING

In this course, you are required to 'explain the difference between binary searching and serial searching, highlighting the advantages and disadvantages of each'. In a serial search, unavoidable when items are in a random order, the search starts at the first item in the list, compares it with the search item and stops if found else the search moves on with each item looked at in turn until either the item is found or the search reaches the end of the list of items.

In a binary search, the middle item in a list is compared with the search item. If it matches the search stops else the search item is either greater than or less than the middle item. The search continues on the half of the list within which the search item may be found. The middle of this list is compared with the search item. If not found the list is again divided into two and the process continues until either the item is found or the search fails. Repeated halving in this fashion results in a search length of n items of no more than $\ln_2 n + 1$ comparisons. This means that for a list of 1000 items the maximum number of search and comparisons made will be $\ln_2 1000 + 1 = 10$. (In simple terms, 1,000 can be halved at most 10 times).

Clearly binary searches are much faster than serial searches for data sets larger than a few items. For instance, a serial search will take an average of 500 comparisons to find an item in a list of 1,000 items. A binary search will take no more than 10. Searching 1,000,000 items, a serial search will take, on average, 500,000 comparisons whereas a binary search will take no more than 20.

However, whereas a serial search can deal with data in a random format, a binary search requires that the data be sorted in some manner. This can often take some time and much time and effort has been expended by computer scientists to develop faster and more efficient sorting algorithms.

A list of cities is Aberdeen, Belfast, Cardiff, Glasgow, Oxford, York. Show the steps of a serial search for York in the list. [F453 Q5 Jan 2010 (2)]

- Start at Aberdeen
- Look at each word in turn/then Belfast, Cardiff etc
- ...until York is found

Show the steps of a binary search for York in the list. (3)

- Look at middle/Cardiff/Glasgow
- York is in second half of list
- Repeated halving
- ...until York is found

Explain one advantage of a binary search compared with a serial search when searching for an item in any large set of data. (2)

- (Usually) faster because
- ...half of data is discarded at each step/fewer items are checked

Show the result of merging the following data files. [F453 Q5 Jun 2010 (2)]

File A : Anna, Cleo, Helen, Pritti
File B : Billy, Ian, Omar, Rob, Tom

Answer: Anna, Billy, Cleo, Helen, Ian, Omar, Pritti, Rob, Tom

The examiner awarded marks on the basis of the following points.

- Correct order
- All names used once

Write an algorithm to merge two sorted files, stating any assumptions you make. (6)

- Open existing files
- Create new file
- Check existing files are not empty
- Use pointers/counters to identify records for comparison
- Repeat
- ...compare records indicated by pointers
- ...copy earlier value record to new file
- ...move correct pointer
- Until end of one file
- Copy remaining records from other file
- Close files

Assumptions

- Assume common key
- Assume if two records are the same
- …only one is written to new file

In this section of the specification, the examiners want you to 'explain the differences between the insertion and quick sort methods, highlighting the characteristics, advantages and disadvantages of each'. The characteristics of both are as follows.

Insertion sort

- Step through the list
- …taking each item in turn and inserting it into its correct position
- …relative to the items before it
- Repeat until all items in the list have been inserted into the correct positions

Quick Sort

- Select an item at random, call this the pivot
- Create two new lists, one with all items less than pivot, other with items greater than pivot
- Repeat until each list only has one item

Insertion sorts are simple to implement, are stable (i.e. elements with the same value retain their relative order after sorting is complete), take little if any additional memory and for small data sets are quicker than a quicksort due in part to the overhead of the recursion calls made by the quicksort. However, for larger lists quicksorts are typically many times faster.

Explain how a quick sort can be used to put a set of numbers into ascending numerical order. You may use the following set of numbers to help explain how the quick sort routine works. [F453 Q5 Jan 2010 (5)]

30 9 46 14 22

	30 →	9	46	14	22 ←
swap 30 & 22	22 →	9	46	14	30 ←
	22	9 →	46	14	30 ←
	22	9	46 →	14	30 ←
swap 46 & 30	22	9	30 →	14	46 ←
	22	9	30 →	14	46 ←
swap 30 & 14	22	9	14 →	30 ←	46
	22	9	14	30 ⇄	46

Split into sublists and repeat.

Marks were awarded for the following points.

- Highlight first number in the list (the search number)
- Pointer at each end of list

- Repeat
- Compare numbers being pointed to
- If in wrong order, swap
- Move pointer of non-search number
- Until pointers coincide so search number in correct position
- Split list into 2 sublists
- Quick sort each sublist
- Repeat until all sublists have a single number
- Put sublists back together

Alternative answer using a pivot:

- Select an item at random, the pivot
- Create two new lists
- ...one with all items less than pivot
- ...other with items greater than pivot
- Repeat
- ...until lists only have one item

On the numbers given, the beginning could be demonstrated by the following diagram.

30	9	46	14	22	pivot is 46
30	9	14	22	46	numbers moved to left of pivot as smaller, choose 14 as new pivot for left section
9	14	30	22	46	30 moved to right of 14 as larger

Describe how an insertion sort is used to arrange the following set of numbers into ascending order. [F453 Q5 Jun 2011 (5)]

17   2   3   26   5

Original set	17	2	3	26	5
Insert 17	17	2	3	26	5
Insert 2	2	17	3	26	5
Insert 3	2	3	17	26	5
Insert 26/no change	2	3	17	26	5
Insert 5	2	3	5	17	26

State one feature of a quick sort which is not used in an insertion sort. (1)

- Set of numbers broken into multiple sets
- Uses pivots

High-level language programming paradigms

6.1 PROGRAMMING PARADIGMS

Low-level invariably refers to assembly languages. There are as many of these as there are different microprocessors, since each microprocessor has its own unique instruction set and consequently its own unique assembly language.

Procedural languages refer to languages such as C, Pascal and Fortran. In these languages data and code are separate. Code is (usually) modularised and programs are a combination of *sequence*, *selection* and *iterative* constructs. Sequence simply means one after the other, selection constructs are normally of the form `if then else` while iterative constructs include statements along the lines of `for (int i = 0; i < 100; i++)` or `while (x < 0) do` or `repeat ...until`. In procedural languages, the programmer specifies the steps needed to execute the program and the order in which they should be carried out.

Object oriented languages such as C++ or Java are direct descendants of procedural languages and add concepts such as *encapsulation*, i.e. data and code are coded together in *classes* and *instantiated* as *objects*. Classes may *inherit* data and methods from other classes. The same methods may be defined numerous times in classes, each method differing from another only in the number of (*overloading*) or types of arguments (*polymorphism*) it takes.

Data encapsulation means that data can only be accessed via methods provided by objects.

A *class* describes shared attributes and methods and acts as a template for a set of objects that have state and behaviour.

An *object* is one instance of a class, often a real-world entity.

Inheritance occurs when a class has its own attributes and methods and also those from its super class.

A *derived class* has all the features of its superclass and has additional features of its own.

A *declarative* language is one in which the program consists of declarations: statements that ← See page 54
specify what properties the results should have. The outcomes are described, but not how they are to be achieved. The order of declarations should not be important.

Describe the difference between declarative languages and procedural languages. [F453 Q6 Specimen Questions (2)]

- Declarative
    - States what is required.
- Procedural
    - Describes how to solve a problem.

High level languages include procedural and object oriented languages. Describe the features of a procedural high level language. [F453 Q6 Jan 2011 (4)]

- Imperative language
- Uses sequence, selection & iteration
- Program states what to do
- ...& how to do it
- Program statements are in blocks
- Each block is a procedure or function max
- Logic of program is given as a series of procedure calls

The table below shows some statements about types of programming language. Tick the boxes to show the type of programming language for which each statement is correct. [F453 Q6 Jun 2010 (5)]

	Low-level	O-O	Procedural
Data is only accessible through methods			
Each instruction usually represents one machine code instruction			
Inheritance may be used			
Local variables may be used			
Mnemonics are used			

Answer:

	Low-level	O-O	Procedural
Data is only accessible through methods		✓	
Each instruction usually represents one machine code instruction	✓		
Inheritance may be used		✓	
Local variables may be used		✓	✓
Mnemonics are used	✓		

6.2   THE UNIFIED MODELLING LANGUAGE

UML is used to specify, visualise, modify, construct and document an object-oriented software-intensive system under development. UML offers a standard way to visualise a system's architectural blueprints, including elements such as:

- activities
- actors
- business processes
- database schemas

- (logical) components
- programming language statements
- reusable software components

UML combines techniques from data modelling (entity relationship diagrams), business modelling (work flows), object modelling, and component modelling. It can be used with all processes, throughout the software development life cycle, and across different implementation technologies[5].

Explain why the Unified Modelling Language (UML) is used. [F453 Q11 Jun 2010 (2)]

- It is a standard way to present information
- …and to illustrate the design of a system
- …in a visual manner, so it is easy to understand
- It allows systems analysts, programmers and clients to communicate
- It makes system maintenance easier
- …when modifying a system

UML diagrams come in various flavours. The diagrams shown below are examples of *class*, *object*, *use case*, *state*, *sequence*, *activity* and *communication* diagrams.

Class diagram

Class diagrams are structure diagrams that describe the structure of a system by showing the system's classes, their attributes, functions(often called operations or methods in O-O) and the relationships between the classes.

Vehicle
name : String noOfDoors : integer …
String getName() int getNoOfDoors() …

This class diagram shows a class `Vehicle` with data item `name` represented as a string and `noOfDoors` as an integer. It also includes the two methods `getName()` which returns a string and `getNoOfDoors()` which returns an integer. The ellipsis in both data and method sections indicate that there are more data items and more methods which have not been shown here.

---

[5]http://en.wikipedia.org/

The UML class diagram shows some of the information about staff working in a health centre.

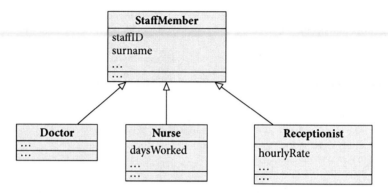

Using the class diagram above, explain the term inheritance. [F453 Q6 Jan 2010 (3)]

- A class that has all the attributes and operations of its superclass
- …and may also have attributes & operations of its own
- E.g. an object of class Nurse has surname from StaffMember
- …in addition to daysWorked

Dr Connor is a doctor at the health centre. From the diagram, explain why his attributes include surname but do not include hourlyRate. (2)

- Dr Connor is an instance of Doctor
- Surname is inherited from StaffMember
- HourlyRate is not an attribute of Doctor or of StaffMember
- HourlyRate is an attribute of Receptionist
- …which is not a superclass for Doctor

Cleaning staff should be included in the class diagram. A cleaner needs the attribute hoursWorked and operation getHours( ). Show this information on a suitable class diagram. (3)

Answer:

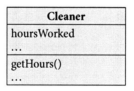

Mrs Jones is employed as a cleaner at the same health centre. The following program code may be used.

```
oneCleaner = Cleaner new
oneCleaner.giveSurname: Jones
```

Use the information given to explain the terms object and class. Give an example of each. (3,3)

Object

- An instance of a class
- A real-world entity
- Holds attributes and methods
- E.g. oneCleaner / Mrs Jones

Class

- A template for
- A set of objects
- ...that have state and behaviour
- E.g. Cleaner/StaffMember/Doctor/Nurse/Receptionist

A council provides a number of public libraries. Information about library staff is to be stored. All staff work at just one library and are paid an annual salary. Their names and contact details must be stored. For each librarian, their qualifications must be stored. One senior librarian is in charge of each library: for this responsibility, they are paid an extra fee. Cleaning staff also work at each library: each cleaner works only on certain days of the week, so the days need to be stored.

Draw a UML class diagram to show the information about library staff. You should include all the information given. [F453 Q6 Jan 2011 (8)]

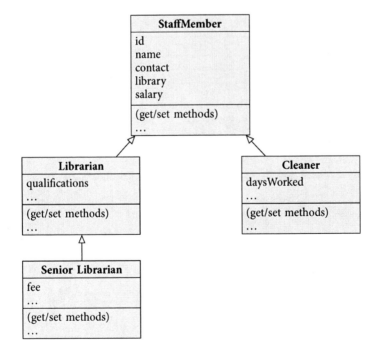

The Universal Modelling Language (UML) class diagram is used to show registered vehicles in this country. The diagram is incomplete.

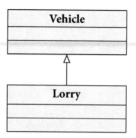

State where the classes Car and Moped should be added to the diagram, and give a reason for your answer. (You may draw on the diagram.) [F453 Q6 Jun 2011 (2)]

- At the same level as Lorry...
- ...as they are subclasses of Vehicle/they inherit

Alternatively

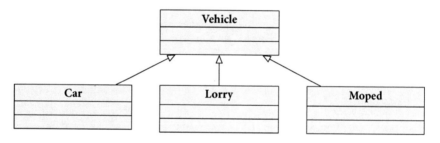

The registration numbers should be stored. State which class should store the registration number and give a reason for your answer. (2)

- Vehicle
- ...as it is the superclass/as other classes are subclasses/as all vehicles have the property

A company sells used cars. Part of the class diagram for UsedCar is shown.

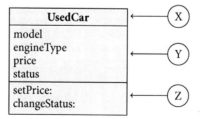

State one method (operation) shown on the diagram. (1)

- setPrice:/changeStatus:

State one attribute (property) shown on the diagram. (1)

- model/engineType/price/status

State in which section of the diagram (X, Y or Z) yearOfManufacture should be shown. (1)

- Y

The following represents a class diagram for a shop with sections labelled X, Y and Z.

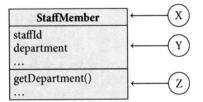

State the meaning of each section of the diagram. [F453 Q10 Specimen Questions (3)]

- X : class name
- Y : attributes for the class
- Z : operations for the class

Explain the meaning of the ellipsis (...) in section Z. (1)

- There are more operations available (the others have been elided)
- This simplifies the diagram
- Only relevant operations are shown

Object diagram

Object diagrams show a complete or partial view of the structure of a modelled system at a specific time.

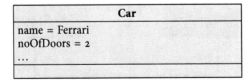

An *anonymous* object which may be used to represent any object in the given class is shown by preceding the name with a colon ':' as in this example.

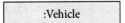

Use case diagram

Use case diagrams are a type of behavioural diagram defined by and created from a Use-case analysis. Their purpose is to present a graphical overview of the functionality provided by a system in terms of actors, their goals (represented as use cases), and any dependencies between those use cases. The main purpose of a use case diagram is to show what system functions are performed for which actor.

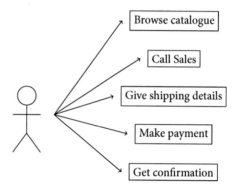

In this example, the actor is running through a typical set of functions in buying something from a catalogue.

State diagram

UML state machine diagrams describe the behaviour of a class over time through illustrations of the states and transitions of a single object progressing through its lifetime. State machine diagrams are a traditional object-oriented way to show behaviour and to document how an object responds to events, including internal and external stimuli.

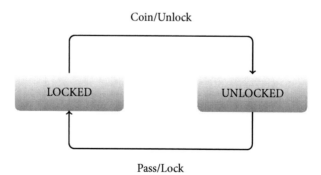

The label on a transition has two parts separated by a slash. The first is the name of the event that triggers the transition. The second is the name of an action to be performed once the transition has been triggered. We can interpret Figure 1 as follows:

- If the turnstile is in the Locked state, and a Coin event occurs, then the turnstile transitions to the Unlocked state, and the Unlock action is performed.
- If the turnstile is in the Unlocked state, and a Pass event occurs, then the turnstile transitions to the Locked state, and the Lock action is performed.

This describes how the turnstile works when things go as planned. Presume that the turnstile begins in the Locked state. When a customer wants to pass through the turnstile they must deposit a coin. This causes the Coin event to occur. The Coin event, in the Locked state, causes the turnstile to transition to the Unlocked state, and causes the Unlock action to be invoked. Next the customer passes through the turnstile. This causes the Pass event to occur. The Pass event, in the Unlocked state, causes the turnstile to go back to the Locked state, and to invoke the Lock action.

The diagram shows details of a used car.

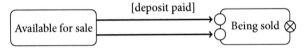

Give the correct name for this type of UML diagram. [F453 Q6 Jun 2011 (1)]

- State diagram

State the meaning of the symbol ◯ (1)

- Entry point

State the meaning of the symbol ⊗ (1)

- Exit point

Sequence diagram

Sequence diagrams are used primarily to show the interactions between objects in the sequential order that those interactions occur. A sequence diagram shows as parallel vertical lines (lifelines), different processes or objects that live simultaneously, and, as horizontal arrows, the messages exchanged between them, in the order in which they occur. This allows the specification of simple runtime scenarios in a graphical manner.

The Unified Modelling Language (UML) sequence diagram shows what happens when a driver uses a remote control key to unlock his car.

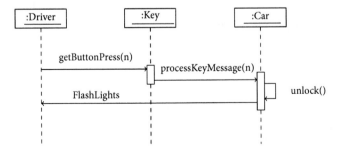

From the diagram, state a message. [F453 Q6 Jan 2011 (1)]

- getButtonPress( )/processKeyMessage( )/unlock( )

A class. (1)

- Driver/Key/Car

A signal. (1)

- FlashLights

Another type of UML diagram included within the sequence diagram. (1)

- Object diagram

Activity diagrams

Activity diagrams show the flow of activities through the system. Diagrams are read from top to bottom and have branches and forks to describe conditions and parallel activities. A fork is used when multiple activities are occurring at the same time.

Below is a possible activity diagram for processing an order. The diagram shows the flow of actions in the system's workflow. Once the order is received the activities split into two parallel sets of activities. One side fills and sends the order while the other handles the billing. On the Fill Order side, the method of delivery is decided conditionally. Depending on the condition either the Overnight Delivery activity or the Regular Delivery activity is performed. Finally the parallel activities combine to close the order.

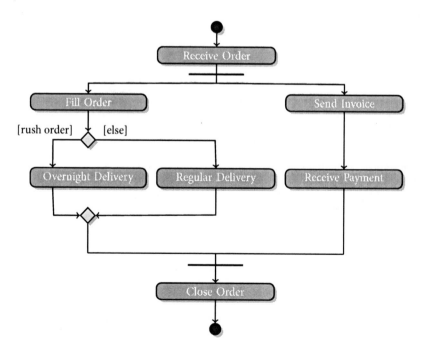

Communication diagrams

Communication diagrams model the interactions between objects or parts in terms of sequenced messages. Communication diagrams represent a combination of information taken from Class, Sequence, and Use Case Diagrams describing both the static structure and dynamic behavior of a system. Communication diagrams show a lot of the same information as sequence diagrams, but because of how the information is presented, some of it is easier to find in one diagram than the other. Communication diagrams show which elements each one interacts with better, but sequence diagrams show the order in which the interactions take place more clearly.

At the entrance to a car park, a car driver has to stop at the barrier and press a button on the ticket machine. The machine issues a ticket to the driver, then raises the barrier to allow the car to enter. This is shown on the UML diagram below. The diagram is incomplete. [F453 Q6 Jan 2011 (1)]

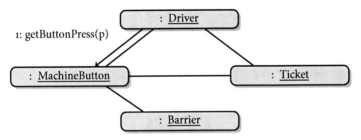

Give the correct name for this type of UML diagram.

- Communication diagram

Add arrows and labels to the diagram above so that it shows the process described. (Do not add extra features which are not in the description.) (3)

Answer:

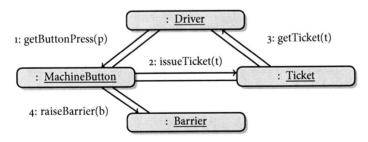

6.3 DECLARATIVE LANGUAGES

A *declarative* language is one in which the program consists of declarations: statements that specify what properties the results should have. The outcomes are described, but not how they are to be achieved. The order of declarations should not be important. An example of such a language is *Prolog*. It is extensively used in artificial and expert systems. Programming in Prolog involves building a *knowledge base* by declaring a large number of "rules" to the system and "facts", then asking the Prolog system to deduce conclusions about the knowledge base. The necessary processing is accomplished by a logical inference machine together with a logic engine program.

A declarative language is a programming language that uses facts and rules where a *fact* is a predicate which may have arguments and is something that is always unconditionally true.

A *rule* is used to define a relationship between facts. It is a simple statement stored in the knowledge base and is true depending on a given condition.

A *goal* is a query to be solved.

Backtracking is an important aspect of any declarative language. It can be defined as

- Follow rules...
- ...towards goal
- If goal fails...
- ...go back to previous match and...
- ...start again
- ...from this point...
- ...towards an alternative goal

Finally, *instantiation* is the replacement of an argument to a predicate by a valid matching object. For example if we had the following code:

```
cat(tom)
dog(bob)
```

and our query was `cat(X)` then X would be instantiated in this example by tom.

Some salient features of a declarative language are that further data can be added when available, there is invariably a large amount of information stored in the knowledge base, the order of storage is irrelevant and at any time the system can explain how it arrived at a particular solution. Typical examples where declarative languages are used would include an expert system such as a medical diagnostic system.

The following statements use a language where facts and rules state what to do but not how to do it.

> **cat (tom)** {i.e. Tom is a cat}
> **cat (leo)**
> **cat (snowy)**
> **mouse (jerry)** {i.e. Jerry is a mouse}
>
> **chases (A, B) if cat (A) and mouse (B)**
> **chases (X, Y)?**

Part of the solution to chases (X, Y)? includes the following steps:

step 1	attempt to solve cat (X)
step 2	finds X = tom
step 3	set X = tom
step 4	attempt to solve mouse (Y)
step 5	finds Y = jerry
step 6	a solution is X = tom, Y = jerry
step 7	attempt to solve cat (X)
step 8	finds X = leo

Give the correct name for this type of programming language. [F453 Q6 Jun 2010 (1)]

- Declarative

Give ONE example of a fact. (1)

- cat (tom) or cat (leo) or cat (snowy) or mouse (jerry)

Give ONE example of a rule. (1)

- chases (A, B) if cat (A) and mouse (B)

Give ONE example of a goal. (1)

- chases (X, Y) ?

Give ONE example of instantiation. (1)

- Set X = tom

Explain the term backtracking and give ONE example of backtracking. (3)

- After finding a solution (to a goal)
- …go back and follow an alternative path
- …to attempt to find another solution
- (After step 6) step 7 is the same as step 1

A declarative language is used to give information about a number of shapes that have straight edges.

flat(A)   {shape A is flat}
flat(B)
solid(C)   {shape C is solid}
equal(A)   {edges of shape A are of equal length}
edges(A,3)   {shape A has 3 edges}
edges(B,4)
triangle(X) := **flat(X), edges(X,3)**

State the meaning of backtracking and instantiation. [F453 Q6 Specimen Questions (1,1)]

Backtracking

- Going back to a previously found successful match

Instantiation

- Giving a variable (in a statement) a value

From the information given, show how any solutions to the query ?Triangle(T) are found. (4)

- T = A, flat(A)
- edges(A,3) succeeds, so A
- T = B, flat(B)
- edges(B,3) fails
- No further definitions for flat

Using the same notation, define the shape pent which is a flat shape with 5 edges of equal length. (3)

- pent (X) :=
- flat(X), equal(X), edges(X,5) [all terms included, in any order]
- Correct notation throughout

Programming techniques

7.1 STRUCTURED PROGRAMMING

Structured programming is a methodical approach to program design that emphasises breaking complex tasks into smaller smaller sub-tasks. *Top down programming* (or *stepwise refinement*) is a particular approach to structured programming. It begins with defining the problem in relatively simple terms. This is then split into sub-tasks which are split again and again until the sub-tasks are small enough to be programmed directly. It is fundamental to this approach that no new ideas that were not in the original design are introduced at any stage of the process. This ensures that the final solution is an accurate implementation of the problem.

The final decomposition of the problem in practical terms leads to the construction of functions and procedures, each of which provide code to handle a particular sub-task. *Functions* are blocks of code which solve a particular sub-task. They are given values by the calling code, they operate on the values, usually using locally defined variables as they do so and they return a single value. *Procedures* are effectively the same but will usually not return any values. In some languages such as Pascal there are both procedures and functions, in others, such as C there is no such distinction - all subroutines are functions. Functions that return nothing are usually declared as `void`.

Breaking complex tasks into smaller sub-tasks and hence functions has a number of major advantages.

- Each function can be coded and tested individually
- Difficult-to-write functions can be given to more experienced programmers
- The interaction between functions can be tested thoroughly before putting them together to solve the original problem
- Groups of functions can be gathered together to form libraries which can be re-used

Explain how functions and procedures may be used to develop a program in a structured way. [F453 Q7 Jun 2010 (2)]

- Each module can be written as a functional procedure...
- ...which can be tested individually
- Library routines
- Code is reusable
- Main program consists of calls to functions/procedures...
- ...which may be nested

Discuss the use of functions, procedures and stepwise refinement in developing programs. (The quality of written communication will be assessed in your answer to this question.) [F453 Q7 Jan 2011 (8)]

As with all questions of this type it is important to get your thoughts clear as to both to what the question is asking and what you think are the important points that you need to make in response. It is then important to try to structure your points clearly and unambiguously.

The examiner was expecting you to cover the following points.

Functions:

- Block of code
- ...which performs a single task/calculation
- Returns a single value
- Uses local variables

Procedure:

- Block of code
- ...which performs a task
- ...which may or may not produce a single value
- Uses local variables

Stepwise refinement:

- Breaks a problem into sections
- ...which become progressively smaller
- ...until each module can be written as a single procedure/function
- Each module can be tested separately
- Library routines can be used

7.2   STANDARD PROGRAMMING TECHNIQUES

A particular high level language uses local variables, global variables and parameters. Discuss and compare the use of local variables, global variables and parameters. (The quality of written communication will be assessed in your answer to this question.) [F453 Q7 Jun 2010 (8)]

The same comments apply as with the previous question. The examiners were expecting the following points.

Local variables:

- A variable defined within one part of program
- ...& is only accessible in that part
- Data contained is lost when execution of that part of program is completed
- The same variable names can be used in different modules

Global variables:

- A variable that is defined at the start of a program

- & exists throughout program
- ...including functions/procedures
- Allows data to be shared between modules
- Overridden by local variables with the same name

Parameters:

- Information about an item of data
- ...supplied to a function or procedure
- Can be passed by reference or by value
- Used as a local variable
- So program can return correctly when procedure has been completed/store return address
- Allows data to be transferred

Explain the term parameter. [F453 Q7 Jan 2011 (3)]

- (Information about) an item of data
- ...supplied to a procedure or function
- May be passed by reference or by value
- Used as a local variable

7.3 STACKS

When a program makes a call to a function or a procedure, the return address and the parameters to the function are pushed onto the stack. The called function pops the parameters off the stack, makes use of them, puts any return value on the stack and at the end of the function, given by a closing brace such as } or by an explicit `return` command automatically pops the return address off the stack into the program counter. Consequently execution continues from the point at which the subroutine was called.

Officially, functions return a single value, procedures return none, one or more, but parameters can be passed by value or by reference. By value means that the actual value of the parameter is put onto the stack, so for example if you made the call to the subroutine `maximum(x,y)` where x and y had previously been initialised to 3 and 4, `maximum` would see the values 3 and 4 on the stack. If, on the other hand the parameters were passed by reference, the addresses of x and y would be passed on the stack. This means that `maximum` can modify the values in those addresses, thus modifying the values of x and y directly. In this way procedures and functions can actually return as many values as the programmer wishes.

As a final comment, recursive routines need to be written very carefully with a terminate condition that is **guaranteed** to be called. Otherwise the stack will grow until the system crashes.

State the type of data structure which is used to handle procedure calling and parameter passing. [F453 Q7 Jan 2011 (1)]

- Stack

State what data structure is used when procedures are called during program execution. [F453 Q7 Jun 2010 (1)]

- Stack

State the purpose of using this data structure. (1)

- So program can return correctly when procedure has been completed/store return address
- Allows data to be transferred

7.4   METHODS FOR DEFINING SYNTAX

Backus-Naur form (BNF) is one way of unambiguously defining the rules of any programming language. Syntax diagrams are another. Defining the rules of the language is clearly essential if the syntax stage of compilation is to run correctly.

State the need for BNF (Backus-Naur form). [F453 Q8 Jun 2010 (1)]

- To unambiguously **define** the syntax of a computer language

In a large company, each employee is given a staff code. Using BNF, the definition of a staff code is

<DIGIT>::= 0 | 1 | 2 | 3 | 4 | 5 | 6 | 7 | 8 | 9
<LETTER>::= A | B | C | D | E
<STAFFCODE>::=<LETTER><DIGIT> | <STAFFCODE><DIGIT>

State how the rules have been broken by each of the invalid staff codes A2C and G45. (1,1)

- A2C : only 1 letter allowed/letter must be at start only
- G45 : G is not defined (as a letter)

After changes in the company, it is decided to allocate new codes. Write a definition for NEWCODE which has one or more digits followed by zero or more letters. For example, 1234 and 3AB are valid but A25 is not valid. (You may assume that DIGIT and LETTER are still defined as earlier.) (3)

Answer:

- < DIGITS>::=<DIGIT>|<DIGIT><DIGITS>
- < LETTERS>::=<LETTER>|<LETTER><LETTERS>
- <NEWCODE>::=<DIGITS>|<DIGITS><LETTERS>

For a particular programming language, the following features are defined:

'digit' is a single digit: 0, 1, 2, 3, 4, 5, 6, 7, 8 or 9
'letter' is any single lower case letter of the alphabet: a, b, c, ... z

The syntax diagram shown below is used to define a variable in the language.

For each of %xy2 and %34, give one reason why the expression is not a variable. [F453 Q8 Jan 2010 (1,1)]

- %xy2 : only 1 letter allowed, this has 2
- %34 : letter missing, there must be one letter

With the help of examples, explain the difference between the following definitions of identifiers. (3)

identifier A

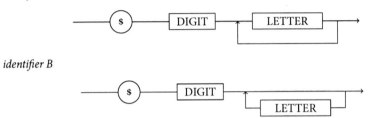

identifier B

- Identifier A must include 1 or more letters
- Identifier B need not include any letters
- E.g. $2 is valid for identifier B but not for identifier A
- ...while $2ab is valid for both

State the purpose of syntax diagrams. [F453 Q7 Jun 2011 (1)]

- To define terms unambiguously (for a computer language)

Give the correct name for another notation that can be used instead of syntax diagrams. (1)

- Backus-Naur Form

Draw a complete set of syntax diagrams to show label where label is a single letter chosen from A, B, C, D or E, followed by the symbol * then any number (including zero) of digits 0, 1, 2, 3, 4, 5, 6, 7, 8, 9.

For example, A*, B*3 and C*456 are labels, but F*7 and DE*8 are not labels. (5)

letter:

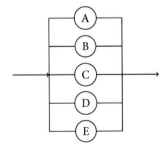

digit:

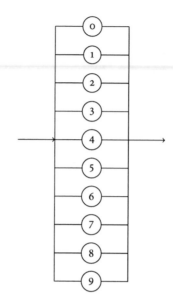

label:

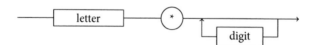

A system uses the following definitions in Backus-Naur form (BNF).

<DIGIT>::= 0 | 1 | 2 | 3 | 4
<ALPHA>::= P | Q | R | S
<CODE>::=<ALPHA><DIGIT> | <ALPHA><CODE>

T3 and PQ23R are not valid codes. From the definitions given, show where the rules have been broken. [F453 Q7 Specimen Questions (1,1)]

T3

- T is not <ALPHA>

PQ23R

- Only one DIGIT is allowed by the definition

Use the BNF definitions from to write a definition for NUMBER, where NUMBER has one or more DIGITs. (2)

- <NUMBER>::=<DIGIT> | <DIGIT><NUMBER> or
- <NUMBER>::=<DIGIT> | <NUMBER><DIGIT>

Draw a syntax diagram to represent the definition of IDENTIFIER, where IDENTIFIER has one ALPHA, then one DIGIT, followed by at least one CODE. Note that you do not have to draw diagrams for LETTER, DIGIT or CODE. (3)

IDENTIFIER

The examiner awarded marks for the following points.

- Definition label
- 3 terms in order
- Correct loop around CODE

7.5 REVERSE POLISH NOTATION

In reverse polish notation, also called postfix notation, operators follow their operands. This eliminates the need for parentheses and is easily implemented using a stack, i.e. ideal for programming algebraic expressions. Operands are pushed onto a stack, operators pop the previous two operands and push the result back onto the stack. At all times, the result of the last calculation is on the top of the stack. This is easy to program and very fast.

The binary tree shows operands p, q and r with operators - and *.

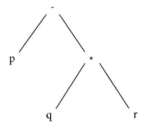

Obtain the reverse Polish form of the expression. [F453 Q7 Jan 2010 (2)]

- Any expression starting with p and using only the terms provided
- pqr*-

State the type of traversal that should be used to obtain the reverse Polish form from a binary tree. (1)

- Post-order (traversal)

An expression in reverse Polish notation is tu*v+ Showing how you obtain your answer, evaluate this expression when t = 2, u = 3 and v = 10. (2)

- Multiply t by u to obtain 6
- Add v to obtain 16

State what data structure, other than a binary tree, may be associated with reverse Polish notation. (1)

- A stack

State a symbol, often used in mathematical expressions, that is not required when working with reverse Polish notation. (1)

- Brackets

The binary tree shows operands a, b and c with operators + and *

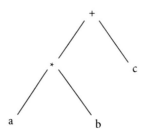

Obtain the reverse Polish form of the expression by using post-order traversal of the tree. [F453 Q7 Specimen Questions (2)]

- ab*c+

An expression in reverse Polish notation is fgh*+. Show how a stack may be used to evaluate this expression when f=3, g=4 and h=5. (4)

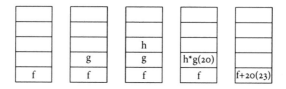

State one advantage of reverse Polish notation compared with the usual (infix) algebraic notation. [F453 Q7 Jun 2011 (1)]

- Any expression can be processed in order (left to right)
- No rules of precedence are needed/no brackets are needed/unambiguous

The binary tree shows operands p, q, r, s with operators *, +,

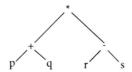

Obtain the reverse Polish form of the expression. (4)

The correct answer is **pq+rs-*** but in the case of incorrect answers, partial marks were awarded for

- An expression starting with pq
- pq+ anywhere in expression
- rs- anywhere in expression

Give the correct name for the type of tree traversal that should be used. (1)

- Post order

8

Low-level languages

8.1 ACCUMULATOR, REGISTERS AND PROGRAM COUNTER

The *accumulator* is a term used to refer to a general purpose register available on every microprocessor that carries out logical and arithmetic instructions. On the early CPUs there was often only a single accumulator. That changed rapidly and in modern CPUs there are many 'accumulators'. Today the term accumulator simply refers to this concept of a useable general purpose register.

A *register* is simply a location in the CPU where data or control information is stored.

Registers that you need to know about include the *Program Counter*, used to hold the address of the next instruction to be executed, the *Memory Address Register (MAR)*, used to hold the address of memory where information is going to be written to or read from, the *Memory Data Register (MDR)*, used to store the data or code that is to be written to or read from the address held in the MAR, the *Current Instruction Register (CIR)*, used to hold the code that is about to be decoded before execution and the *Flags* register within which each bit has a specific meaning.

Purely for interest's sake, to give you some indication of what is in the modern CPU, the following information is taken from the Intel manual "Intel 64 and IA-32 Architectures Software Developers Manual Volume 1: Basic Architecture". You will **NOT** be tested on this :)

Basic program execution registers — The eight general-purpose registers, the six segment registers, the EFLAGS register, and the EIP (instruction pointer) register comprise a basic execution environment in which to execute a set of general-purpose instructions. These instructions perform basic integer arithmetic on byte, word, and doubleword integers, handle program flow control, operate on bit and byte strings, and address memory.

x87 FPU registers — The eight x87 FPU data registers, the x87 FPU control register, the status register, the x87 FPU instruction pointer register, the x87 FPU operand (data) pointer register, the x87 FPU tag register, and the x87 FPU opcode register provide an execution environment for operating on single-precision, double-precision, and double extended-precision floating-point values, word integers, doubleword integers, quadword integers, and binary coded decimal (BCD) values.

MMX registers — The eight MMX registers support execution of single- instruction, multiple-data (SIMD) operations on 64-bit packed byte, word, and doubleword integers.

XMM registers — The eight XMM data registers and the MXCSR register support execution of SIMD operations on 128-bit packed single-precision and double- precision floating-point values and on 128-bit packed byte, word, doubleword, and quadword integers.

So, plenty of registers to play with in the modern CPU.

Explain the purpose of the accumulator.

- Temporary storage (within ALU)
- Holds data being processed/used during calculations
- Deals with the input and output in the processor

8.2   IMMEDIATE, DIRECT, INDIRECT, RELATIVE AND INDEXED ADDRESSING

Many assembly language instructions act upon memory in some way. These instructions contain an address field that contain information about which memory location the instruction should use. This field can be used in a number of ways.

Immediate addressing - the data in the address field holds a constant needed by the program. An example in Intel x86 code might be mov eax,#4 which loads the eax register with the number 4.

Direct addressing - the data in the address field holds the address of the memory location whose contents are required. E.g. mov eax,1234 copies whatever is in address 1234 into the eax register.

Indirect addressing - the data in the address field holds the address of a memory location which itself is holding the address of a memory location that is holding the value we want. The following diagram should hopefully make this clear.

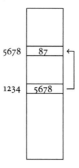

In this diagram, memory address 1234 is shown holding the value 5678. Address 5678 is shown holding the value 87. Consequently executing the instruction mov eax, [1234] will cause the contents of address 1234, i.e. 5678 to be treated as an address and the contents of this address, i.e. 87 to be copied into the eax register.

Indexed addressing - uses a base address from an index register and an offset to load data. Let us suppose that the base pointer index register `esi` holds the value 1000. The instruction `mov,eax,esi+2` will add 1000 to 2, getting 1002 and will then cause the contents of whatever is at address 1002 to be copied into the `eax` register. Indexed addressing is commonly used to access the contents of data structures such as arrays.

Relative addressing - let us suppose that we are writing a program which typically has a few dozen variables, some arrays and a few more complex data structures. When the compiler and linker have finished their job, all of these data items are given addresses relative to the start of the data area set aside by the linker. For example if we are using an integer variable `myPeopleCount` to refer to the number of people who voted in the recent school election, the linker might have given `myPeopleCount` address 20 relative to the start of the data area. When the program is loaded into memory, the loader will allocated a suitable piece of memory specifically for the data area and will tell the program where the data area starts. If for example, the loader puts the data area at absolute address 2AB4DC04 in RAM, the absolute address of `myPeopleCount` would now be at 2AB4DC04+20=2AB4DC18 but since the code in the executable file refers to `myPeopleCount` by its address relative to the start of the data area it is of no consequence what its absolute memory address is.

Similarly, after the compiler and linker have finished converting your program written in high level code into machine code, unless specifically indicated otherwise all memory addresses and calls and jumps to functions made in the code will be relative to the call or jump point. So if for example, the code makes a call to your special function `addMoreVotes` the assembly language instruction will call (i.e. jump, but later return) an address that is relative to where it the call instruction is in memory. If for example the instruction `call 2000` is found in the machine code of your program, this will mean to call the code found 2000 bytes further along the code. Absolute addressing is pretty much forbidden in modern operating systems.

State the type of addressing described in each of the following.

Add the number 13 to the contents of the accumulator. [F453 Q8 Specimen Questions (1)]

- Immediate

Add the number stored in address 25 to the contents of the accumulator. (1)

- Direct

Describe the use and purpose of the index register. (3)

- Stores a number used to modify the address in the address field (or data) of an instruction
- Used in indexed addressing
- Allows access to a range of memory locations
- E.g. used to access an array

State the meaning of direct addressing. (1)

- The instruction gives the address to be used

Explain why it is not possible to use only direct addressing in assembly languages. (1)

- The number of addresses available is limited

- ...by the size of the address field
- Code is not relocatable/code uses fixed memory locations

Describe relative addressing. [F453 Q9 Jun 2010 (3)]

- Allows a real address to be calculated...
- ...from a base address...
- ...by adding the relative address
- Relative address is an offset
- Can be used for arrays
- Can be used for branching

Describe indexed addressing. (3)

- Modifies the address given
- ...by adding the number
- ...from the index register
- ...to address in instruction

One feature of assembly language is flow-control. Explain the term flow-control. (2)

- The order in which instructions are executed
- The order may be changed by a jump instruction/conditional jump instruction

Describe immediate addressing. [F453 Q8 Jan 2011 (2)]

- Used in assembly language
- Uses data in address field
- ...as a constant

Explain how and why the index register (IR) is used. (3)

- Used in indexed addressing
- Stores a number used to modify an address
- ...which is given in an instruction
- Allows efficient access to a range of memory locations/by incrementing the value in the IR
- E.g. used to access an array

Describe how a jump instruction is executed.

- By changing contents of PC (to address part of instruction)
- Copy address part of instruction
- ...in CIR to PC

8.3   Mnemonics, opcode and symbolic addressing

An assembly language uses mnemonics. Explain the term mnemonics. [F453 Q9 Jun 2010 (2)]

- A code that is easily remembered ...
- ...used to give the opcode/instruction
- E.g. ADD

In the context of assembly languages, state the meaning of the term opcode (operation code) and operand [F453 Q8 Specimen Questions (3)]

- Opcode : The (mnemonic) part of the instruction that indicates what it is to do
- Operand : The data part of the instruction

A program in a particular assembly language includes the instructions

```
        JMP CD ; jump to instruction labelled CD

CD      ADN 41 ; add 41 to the accumulator
```

Explain the term opcode and give one example from the information given. [F453 Q8 Jan 2010 (2)]

- The mnemonic part of the instruction/that indicates what it is to do/code for the operation
- JMP or ADN

State the type of addressing used by the instruction ADN 41. (1)

- Immediate

State the meaning of the term symbolic addressing and give one example from the information given. (2)

- The use of characters to represent the address of a store location, i.e. CD

Explain the use of an operand in an assembly language instruction. [F453 Q8 Jun 2011 (4)]

- Address field (in an instruction)
- It holds data
- ...to be used by the operation given in the opcode
- E.g. in ADD 12, 12 is the operand

Describe direct addressing and indirect addressing, making clear the difference between them. You may use diagrams. (6)

Direct:

- The simplest/most common method of addressing
- Uses the (data in) the address field
- ...without modification
- E.g. In ADD 23, use the number stored in address 23 for the instruction
- Limits the memory locations that can be addressed

Indirect:

- Uses the address field as a vector/pointer
- ...to the address to be used
- Used to access library routines
- E.g. In ADD 23, if address 23 stores 45, address 45 holds the number to be used
- Increases the memory locations that can be addressed

Databases

9.1 FLAT FILES AND RELATIONAL DATABASES

Flat-file databases

- Keep all the records are in one table
- Each row in the table corresponds to one record
- Each column in the table corresponds to a different field.
- Tables are two-dimensional structures

This means that

- Duplicate data is stored
- …so storage is wasted, i.e. data redundancy
- Data is often inconsistent
- …because there may be more than one version of the data item
- Everything is interlinked
- …so it is difficult to change the data format
- Changes to data
- …may require rewriting the entire file
- Lack of flexibility
- …therefore it is difficult to obtain new types of reports

Relational databases on the other hand

- Keep data as a number of related tables
- …thus avoiding data duplication
- …and inconsistent data
- It is easier to change data
- It is easier to change the data format
- Data can be added easily
- It is easier to control access to data

9.2 3NF USING ENTITY-RELATIONSHIP DIAGRAMS AND DECOMPOSITION

Normalisation is the process by which many-many relationships are replaced and duplicate data is avoided. *Third normal form* contains no functional dependencies between attributes other than the primary key, it limits duplication of data and it removes multi-valued attributes.

Entity relationship diagrams are diagrams which show how entities are related to one another. The relationships between entities are either one to one, one to many, many to one or many to many. These are indicated in an entity relationship diagram by the use of lines joining the entities. The four possibilities are shown below.

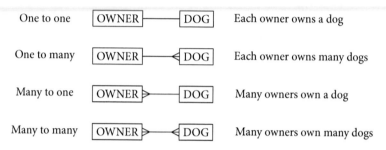

Many to many relationships are not acceptable in 3NF and a new entity whose name is often an amalgam of the two entities currently in the many to many relationship is inserted between the two entities. The new entity forms a one-many relationship with the entity to its left and a many to one relationship with the entity to its right. The diagram below shows how this is done.

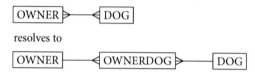

Customers of a classical music shop are able to register their details and buy CDs from the shop's website. The entity-relationship (E-R) diagram below shows

CUSTOMERFINANCE	includes customers bank details
CUSTOMER	includes name and address
ORDER	details of a customer order, including the date
CD	data about a CD, as described earlier

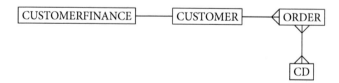

State the type of relationship between CUSTOMERFINANCE and CUSTOMER on the E-R diagram above. [F453 Q10 Jun 2010 (1)]

- One-to-one

Give ONE reason why CUSTOMERFINANCE and CUSTOMER are stored separately. (1)

- Security/privacy/different access rights to sensitive data

Explain ONE reason why CUSTOMER and ORDER are stored separately. (2)

- A customer may have multiple orders
- Separate storage avoids data duplication
- Avoids data inconsistency

State ONE problem with the relationship between ORDER and CD on the diagram. (1)

- Many-many/not in 3rd Normal Form (3NF)

Draw an improved version of the E-R diagram which corrects this problem. (3)

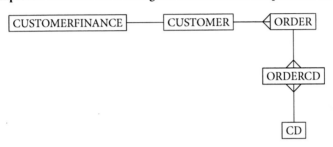

An animal hospital is run by a team of vets. Owners may take their pets for treatment at any time. A relational database is used to store all the data needed in the hospital. Data is stored about pets and their owners. Each pet has only one owner, but an owner may have one or more pets. Complete an entity-relationship (E-R) diagram to show this relationship. [F453 Q9 Jan 2010 (2)]

Draw an entity-relationship (E-R) diagram to show the following:

> **A to B is a one-one relationship**
> **B to C is a one-many relationship**
> **A to D is a many-one relationship** [F453 Q9 Jan 2011 (4)]

Answer

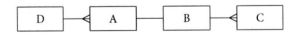

The examiners awarded marks according to the following points.

- A and B linked correctly
- B and C linked correctly
- A and D linked correctly
- No additional entities or relationships and all on one diagram with boxes

A school uses a relational database. Information is stored about students and subjects.State the relationship between the Student and Subject tables. [F453 Q10 Jun 2011 (1)]

- Many-many

Alternatively, the examiners would accept an E-R diagram such as the following.

Explain the consequences of this relationship. (3)

- Not allowed/not in 3NF
- Needs another table between Student & Subject
- ...to avoid duplication of data/to change to 3NF

The relationship of Student to PersonalTutor is shown on the entity-relationship (E-R) diagram.

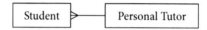

State the relationship shown. (1)

- Many-one

An advertising company produces advertisements for clients. Data is stored in a relational database. When a client wants to launch a new product or improve sales, a campaign is prepared. The campaign may include a number of adverts for television, radio and magazines. Different adverts for a product may use the same media items (e.g. video clips, music, photos). This is shown on the entity-relationship (E-R) diagram.

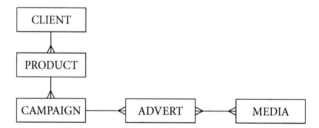

From the diagram, describe the relationship between CAMPAIGN and ADVERT. [F453 Q9 Specimen Questions (1)]

- One-many
- I.e. One Campaign has one or more Adverts, but each Advert is for only one Campaign

Draw this E-R diagram in third normal form (3NF). (3)

Answer

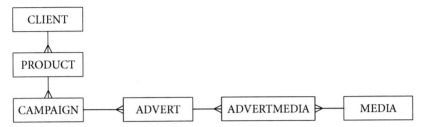

Marks were awarded for the following points.

- Only one named link entity, correctly inserted between Advert and Media
- Correct relationships around ADVERTMEDIA
- All other relationships correct

9.3 Primary, secondary and foreign keys

Definitions

- Entity - a thing about which there is a need to record data
- Attribute - a property of an entity
- Primary key - a unique value which identifies a record
- Secondary key - a unique value which enables a table to be accessed in a different order
- Foreign key - a primary key from one table used as an attribute in another table. It is used primarily to link tables

Continuing from the last question in the previous example, the database designer considers including the following attributes in the tables used for PRODUCT and CAMPAIGN.

PRODUCT (ProdId, ProdName ...)
CAMPAIGN (CampaignId, ClientId, ProdId, Fee, StartDate ...)

Define the term primary key. [F453 Q9 Specimen Questions (1)]

- Unique identifier in a table

Give one example of a primary key in this database. (1)

- ProdId in Product/CampaignId in Campaign

Explain why ClientId (from the CLIENT table) should not be included in the CAMPAIGN table. (2)

- Transitive dependency, so knowing the ProdID, ClientId can be determined
- Campaign is related to Client via Product
- If ClientId were included in Campaign, the database would not be in 3NF.

An animal hospital is run by a team of vets. A relational database is used to store all the data needed in the hospital. Data is stored about pets and their owners. Each pet has only one owner, but an owner may have one or more pets. Data stored includes the following

PET (PetId, Name, Breed, Colour,...)
OWNER (OwnerId, Surname, Forename, ...)

Explain the use of primary keys in this database. [F453 Q9 Jan 2010 (2)]

- Unique identifier
- E.g. PetId in PET
- E.g. OwnerId in OWNER

Explain the use of a foreign key in this database. (3)

- Primary key from one table
- ...used as an attribute in another
- ...to link tables/provide relationship between tables
- E.g. OwnerId stored in PET
- ...shows who owns each pet

A shop sells classical music CDs. Data stored is stored in a relational database and stored information about each CD includes the name of the composer, the title, the name of the artiste or orchestra, the price and the number in stock. State why the name of the composer is NOT suitable as a primary key. [F453 Q10 Jun 2010 (1)]

- Not unique/more than one CD with same composer

Explain the use of a secondary key from the information given. (2)

- Used to search for a group of records
- E.g. CDs with same artiste

State the meaning of the term primary key. [F453 Q9 Jan 2011 (1)]

- Unique identifier (in a table)

Explain why a foreign key is also a primary key, but a primary key need not be a foreign key. (4)

- Foreign key links tables (to represent many to one relationship)
- ...so that only one record is accessed/to avoid duplicate data
- E.g. primary key from B used as foreign key in C
- Primary key is in a table that may contain data not required in another table
- E.g. primary key from C is not used in B and hence cannot be a foreign key

The relationship of Student to PersonalTutor is shown on the entity-relationship (E-R) diagram.

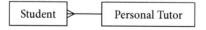

Explain the use of primary and foreign keys for Student and PersonalTutor. [F453 Q10 Jun 2011 (5)]

- Both tables have their own primary key
- ...which is a unique identifier
- Primary key from PersonalTutor
- ...is used as an attribute in Student
- ...and as a foreign key in Student
- ...and used to create the relationship/link between tables

State the meaning of the term secondary key and give an example of the use of a secondary key in the school database described. (2)

Meaning:

- (An attribute that) can be used to search for a group of records
- ...or allows records to be accessed in a different order

Example:

- E.g. search for TutorId in Student to find all students with a particular personal tutor
- E.g. StudentSurname in Student can access students in alphabetical order

9.4 THE DBMS

A database management system (DBMS) is software that can find data in a database, add new data and change existing data. A DBMS may provide its own simple user interface, or more commonly, communicate with external programs using a *data manipulation language (DML)*. The most common of these today is *Structured Query Language (SQL)*. The description of which data items are stored together with the relationships between them are written in a *data description language (DDL)*. The DDL defines the schema, creates tables, create attributes, defines data types, primary and foreign keys and the validation rules. Many systems today use XML and/or SQL as their DDL. The *data dictionary* is a file containing descriptions of, and other information about, the structure of the data held in the database.

A database management system (DBMS) uses a data description language (DDL) and a data manipulation language (DML). Each statement given below may apply to a DDL, a DML or both. Tick one box in each row to show which is correct. [F453 Q9 Jan 2011 (7)]

	DDL only	DML only	Both DDL & DML
It is used to create new tables			
It defines foreign keys			
It can query data			
It can sort data into an order			
It is used to update the data			
It is a high level language			
It is used for writing the schema			

Answer:

	DDL only	DML only	Both DDL & DML
It is used to create new tables	✓		
It defines foreign keys	✓		
It can query data		✓	
It can sort data into an order		✓	
It is used to update the data		✓	
It is a high level language			✓
It is used for writing the schema	✓		

A database management system (DBMS) includes a data dictionary. Explain the term data dictionary and give two examples of the information stored. [F453 Q9 Jan 2010 (4)]
Description

- A file containing descriptions of data in database
- ...used by database managers
- ...when altering database structure
- Uses metadata to define the tables

Examples

- Names of tables/columns
- Characteristics of data (e.g. length, data type)
- Restrictions on values in columns
- Meaning of data columns
- Relationships between data
- ...which programs can access data
- Identifies primary keys
- Identifies foreign keys
- Identifies indexes
- Defines access rights

Relational databases can be used to produce reports. Explain the term report and state two features, other than report layout, included in a report definition. [F453 Q10 Jun 2011 (4)]

- Presentation of selected data
- ...usually in the form of a table/specific layout
- May be defined in advance
- ...so the user does not need to set it up

Features

- A query
- A display order

Give two reasons why views of data are made available to users of a database. [F453 Q9 Jan 2011 (2)]

- So users can access the data they need
- Users do not need specialist knowledge
- To protect data
- To prevent unauthorised access

A pet shop has decided to start selling pet toys. Details of toys and their suppliers need to be added to the current relational database. State the type of language used to create the table TOY. [F453 Q9 Jan 2011 (1)]

- Data description language/DDL

9.5 USING SQL

Query languages are relatively simple languages designed specifically to allow users to query and more generally manage data in relational databases. Structured Query Language (SQL) is a very popular example of one of these languages and in its inclusion in the open source relational database management system, MySQL, is used to power dynamic sites across the world wide web.

SQL is most commonly used to query relational databases. The `SELECT` statement is used to select data from one or more tables. SQL has a number of clauses, some of which are as follows.

The `FROM` clause indicates which table(s) are to be interrogated.
`WHERE` clause indicates comparisons which are used to restrict data returned by the query.
The `GROUP BY` clause groups returned data into appropriate classes.
The `ORDER BY` clause identifies how the returned data is to be sorted.

An asterisk * is used to specify that the query should return all data matching the query.

Examples

1. To select all chairs from a database where the price is in excess of £1,000.

```
SELECT * FROM Chairs WHERE price > £1,000;
```

2. To display the manufacturer and country of origin of all chairs in the database whose price is in excess of £1,000 ordering by price in descending order.

```
SELECT manufacturer,country
   FROM Chairs
   WHERE price > £1,000
   ORDER BY price DESC;
```

The Data Manipulation Language (DML) is a subset of SQL and is used to add, delete and update data.

`INSERT` adds rows to an existing table.
`UPDATE` modifies rows in an existing table.
`DELETE` deletes rows from an existing table.

Examples

1. To insert into our a table of chairs the manufacturer, 'Eames', country of origin, 'UK', name, 'Lounge chair' and price, '£500'.

```
INSERT INTO Chairs
    (manufacturer,country,name,price)
VALUES
    ('Eames','UK','Lounge chair','500');
```

2. To update our chair table so that manufacturer 'Eames' has the correct country of origin.

```
UPDATE Chairs
  SET country='USA'
  WHERE manufacturer='Eames';
```

3. To delete all of our Charles Eames chairs from the database.

```
DELETE FROM Chairs
  WHERE manufacturer='Eames';
```

Of course we can also use SQL to create and delete databases and tables.

Examples

1. To create our database of furniture.

```
CREATE DATABASE Furniture;
```

2. To create a table Chairs with some suitable fields.

```
CREATE TABLE Chairs (
    chairID int,
    name varchar(50),
    manufacturer varchar(50),
    country varchar(50),
    price real
);
```

3. To delete our database of furniture.

```
DROP DATABASE Furniture;
```

4. To delete our table of chairs.

```
DROP TABLE Chairs;
```

Structured Query Language (SQL) is used with databases. In a supermarket, the following SQL may be used.

SELECT StockNo, Quantity, Price FROM Stock
WHERE Quantity < 100
ORDER BY Price DESC

From this, state the name of one attribute. [F453 Q9 Jan 2011 (1)]

- StockNo/Quantity/Price

State the name of one table. (1)

- Stock

Describe the purpose of the code. (3)

- Lists (values of) attributes StockNo, Quantity & Price in the Stock table
- …for all Stock with (quantity) less than 100 remaining
- …in order of Price from highest to lowest/descending order of Price

SQL is also used to create an employee table in the database. A simplified version of part of this is shown below, with line numbers added.

Line 1   CREATE TABLE Employee
Line 2   (StaffId CHAR(6),
Line 3   Surname VARCHAR(15),
Line 4   Forename VARCHAR(15),
Line 5   DepartmentId CHAR(5),
Line 6   PRIMARY KEY StaffId,
Line 7   FOREIGN KEY DepartmentId REFERENCES Department)

Explain the difference between CHAR and VARCHAR data types in lines 2 and 3. (2)

- CHAR is fixed length
- VARCHAR is variable length

Explain lines 5 and 7. (3)

- Line 5 defines DepartmentId as an attribute (of Employee)/DepartmentId is set at 5 characters
- Line 7 defines DepartmentId as the same attribute in the Department table.
- …where it is the primary key
- …used to link the tables

Some of the Structured Query Language (SQL) used for a particular database is

SELECT CustomerId, AmountOwed, CreditLimit
FROM CUSTOMERFINANCE
WHERE AmountOwed > £80
ORDER BY CreditLimit

Describe the purpose of this code. [F453 Q10 Jun 2010 (3)]

- Lists attributes CustomerId, AmountOwed, and CreditLimit

- ...for all customers who owe more than 80
- ...in order of CreditLimit from lowest to highest

The following shows some of the Structured Query Language (SQL) used to obtain data from a relational database.

SELECT CampaignId, ProdId, Fee, StartDate
FROM CAMPAIGN
WHERE Fee > 20000
ORDER BY Fee DESC;

Describe the purpose of this code. [F453 Q9 Specimen Questions (3)]

- Lists attributes CampaignId, ProdId, Fee and StartDate
- ...for all Campaigns that had fees of more than £20000
- ...in order of Fee from highest to lowest

Index